MW01230813

The True Story

of

FRANCES, THE FALCONER'S DAUGHTER

Wife of

WILLIAM DUNGAN, Gentleman, of London

and of

JEREMY CLARKE, Gentleman, of England & Newport, R. I.

and of

REV. WILLIAM VAUGHAN of Newport

———

THE MOTHER OF GOVERNORS

1607 - 1677

Including Important Events in the Lives of
The Quakers and the Indians

from

Histories and Records
Strung Together with a Few Side Remarks by
Elizabeth Nicholson White

PROVIDENCE

1932

PRIVATELY PRINTED FOR
ELIZABETH NICHOLSON WHITE
AT PROVIDENCE, BY THE
ROGER WILLIAMS PRESS,
E A. JOHNSON COMPANY

FRANCES WAS ALWAYS BUSY WITH HER CHILDREN

Drawn by Helen Mason Gross

FRANCES

THE FALCONER'S DAUGHTER

HER FRIENDS AND CONTEMPORARIES

To My Beloved Brother

SAMUEL MOWRY NICHOLSON

IF this little book can produce an interest in our brave Colonial Mothers, even through criticism the author will be only thankful. If it makes the reader annoyed, so much the better. If it makes the American women, even two or three of them, encouraged to brave the battles of life today by reading of the constancy and devotion to the home and rearing of children, the spirit of the Colonial Mother may well be joyful over her victories. For the women of 1638-77 had as hard tasks as any of the women of any time. By the Grace of God and the Council of His Holy Spirit, they reared leaders, both men and women.

All the facts, names, dates from histories and records—From Colonial Records of R. I., Justins Dungan and Clarke Families; American Encyclopedia, Westerly Records, Newport Records, Sir Wm. Alexander The American Colonization, Prince Society, Richmonds History of Newport, and others.

PART ONE

Being the Side Remarks—Impressions Received by the Author While in the Heart of the Old World Where So Many Evidences of War Are to be Seen.

Impressions from the Old World

ONCE upon a time, in a land of Nowhere and Everywhere, that is to say, in a place which is in no place, yet, in every place!—How can I tell you about it! There are no words to describe it, for it does not belong to us with our limited time and distance and thought! In the Everlasting Illimitable and Unconceivable Kingdom, beyond, above, around us, yet unseen, unknown as yet—

Once there happened, something very much more wonderful than ever had happened before or since. The King was greatly disturbed. There on the little round dirty ball, flying around the great fiery sun, the greatest commotions and splutterings were occurring. In this wonderful harmony of grand music, which the other great balls of fire and of substance made, each humming its own tune and making one varied continual symphony throughout the limitless creation around the King's throne, there was this one discordant horrible noise! One after another of the King's messengers flew off at His bidding to warn the creatures on Earth to cease their dreadful sounds and quarrellings; but one by one they returned, scorned and with wounded hearts and broken wings, to tell their same story of contempt and insult to the King. At last the King's Son, more fair and beautiful than any created thing in the whole Universe, offered to go Himself on the long and painful journey from the Eternal to the Earth. It meant a tremendous amount of preparation. The legions of the King were sent ahead to prepare everything for such a sublime act. All over the Earth they set the creatures to work. There must be roads for these beings to run from place to place with the great news. The roads had to be built in their language, which was warlike, in order to carry the message of the Prince of Peace. These creatures were so contrary.

The Prince was to enter the horrible war-distracted, sin-sick, soul-troubled earth, as a poor, humble, helpless infant. A perfect maiden must be prepared to receive this Great Visitor. He, whom the heavenly spheres rotated continually around, must become obscure, humble, poor and helpless. Ages past He had offered Himself ("Here Am I," "Send Me") to the King. Through his endless, eternal, limitless love, He was to change the tune of din, shrieks and groans of war, to the note designed for the Earth to play. His voice alone, His love alone, His blood alone, could save the world for the King. The inhabitants of this world could not listen, deafened by the wild yellings of their distraught souls! "Peace!" He cried, "Be still." Only in the quiet could they hear His guiding voice. That was two thousand years ago, nearly, as we reckon time. It seems hopeless. It seems as if nothing had improved. But come with me to the

hills of France and see if it isn't more than wonderful, the way it marches on to the culmination.

St. Martin d'Uriage

Very near the Border of three countries there is
a village on a shoulder of a high hill, which by
great steps of hills, finally grows into the side of
one of the greatest mountains, the Bella Donna. It
looks so easy to get to the snow, glistening in the
sun, on top of this peak. Not so far below on the
horizon is a green velvet curved top with a cross
outlined against the blue of the limitless space.

Here in the village every morning the sound of
the bells informs the sleepy heads that it is time for
Mass. Then the great church clock strikes five, and
the lower bell strikes again, five o'clock. A dear old
couple leads their precious cow off over the hills to
the pasture. Two little girls with their pretty fair
hair braided, lead the mother ewe and the three
snow white lambs across the village square over the
path to their safe fields. The daily house-cleaning,
rinsing of the linen, and tending the fields with
their hay or grain fills the morning, till it's time
for the long bread loaf to be cut and eaten with
"potage" and wine—and cheese of various kinds.
Everything looks so well cared for, so peaceful and
contented. Yet they carry the same kind of scythes
and cycles that stormed the Bastille, 140 years
ago; descendants of the same "paysans" who could

countenance the decapitation of the Royalists! People, proud in their integrity, satisfied with their beloved land and customs, with a hatred for luxury and false standards and foreign ideas of all kinds—yet with deepest veneration for the truth. Look out on the horizon. Carved in rock against the sky, lies the huge profile of Napoleon with his hat drawn down over his ears. Here he lies held fast in the rock; he who led his hundreds of thousands of young men to conquer everything for France; here he must lie till Judgment Day.

Wars! Wars and more wars! But that was just yesterday. The mountains tell much more than that! Here, a few minutes walk below us, still stands the perfect chateau, perched on the side of the hill above Uriage.

Just a few years ago, workmen digging through the accumulation of rubbish, found the skeleton of a Turk who had been killed centuries ago when the Saracens attacked and were repelled by the French there. Molten lead—used in the name of Christ, the "Prince of Peace!" It was the only language they knew, even then. War! Say it with fire, death and destruction. It has taken a long time to understand the King's language. Like little restless, growing boys of five or six, they must carry on the Kingdom in military, bombastic style—these creatures.

Over on the west side of the Isère river, which winds like a silver serpent between the mountains and the hills of the East, and the magnificent range of mountains on the West, is a shaft of rock which looks as though, perhaps a thousand or so years ago, a city had been built along its top, where some mighty race of beings, half men and half gods, had lived. Half the time, this stony plateau is above the clouds—and no earthly creatures can tell what these beings may have been like. Only now and then we get glimpses of them through the legends of Greece and Germany and Norway!

GRAND CHARTREUSE

Away off in the interior, twenty miles above the river, along the high road to the Grand Chartreuse, there is the story, in rock, of another great War. For here, concealed far away in the mountain fastness, a powerful group of men, sick of the sins of the world, spent their remaining days in preparing for Death, praying for the sinners of the World; fighting against the enemies of the Soul—Pride, Lust, Hatred, Ease; each day digging a spadeful of their own graves; silent except for the one sentence, "Brother, you must die." Our imagination is baffled in trying to picture conditions which could produce such a reaction. Miles above, on top of the solid wall of rock extending for miles as a background, on the roughest and highest jagged point, stands the Cross! The symbol of the King's Son. What has that to do with monasteries? He lived among the people, daily walking and talking with them, and only for forty days went off to the wilderness, to return again and die, with His people all around Him.

Alas, the cordial brewed by these monks is no longer made there. But it is not the liquor! It is the perfume that tells about the old, old St. Bruno. The remembrance, the fragrance that is in the glass after the vulgar substance has left. The soul of the Saint lingers amid the little old chambers and in the Star garden. The Cross, high up, miles above the Convent. The eternal war against the World, the Flesh and the Devil. The immeasurable depth of sadness in the soul of St. Bruno, which could find peace only in this exalted, isolated fastness. What had the World shown to his pure soul that could have caused such a retreat. Terrible bloody conflicts between the Lords and Barons—between the Christians and Saracens—in the name of Christ. Here he could meditate and pray for the souls of the sinners of the world. Here in his little bare room he could write and study about his Savior. Here he could think out some way to counterbalance the evil of the great cities, by the holy, consecrated life. Here make way for Death, the usher of every living soul to Life Everlasting, or Regrets Eternal. Just a bit of this Soul still lingers through the long stone corridors and massive rooms—in the various chapels and splendid stairways; only the fragrance and memory.

The pine trees tower one above another, moss hung, and wearing peaked caps like an army of sad-faced monks with their cowls drawn over their faces, for mourning the sins of the world. You can hear their moans on cold, dark, windy nights. In vain did the monks of Chartreuse mow the circle of grass to do away with the serpents of the Evil One. In vain did they set fire to the brush-wood and joyfully behold the jumping, agonizing vipers—symbolizing for them the great purification. The monks are gone. The Evil continues. In vain they dug their own graves, little by little, day by day. Death continues. Life is to live. It is not death to die. We die daily. One more glass of the true wine, which St. Bruno found away up in his mountain, with the rushing turbulent stream beside him, with the huge boulders, where the trees grow from green carpets of moss, with birds chanting in the treetops! But alas, his followers, like the world, grew material instead of Spiritual. Even though the Heavenly Dove is painted on the ceiling of the great room, one feels the stone. In the kitchen one sees the huge stones, set not for an altar, but for great feasts—such huge platters and knives, and rooms for the servants to eat in—all far removed from St. Bruno's spirit. But in the little Star garden, there lingers yet his memory. He looked to the Star of the Heaven for that pattern — the Three in One Star of Eternal Hope.

These monasteries were growing all over France till the Twelfth Century, when Cathedrals were at their high-water mark. But first, the desire for a detached life seems to have been given men, before they could raise the heavy lump of humanity.

It seems a little bit like the desire to go and found a new order in America, which filled the hearts and heads of so many, and especially in Newport, Rhode Island, though not through the monasteries, but through covenants.

We, who today might go without starches and sweets to keep from "losing our figures" have no idea of the clear heads which could contemplate for hours without any food, the celestial food on the altars. Even so in Newport there assembled a Society of Friends, who could sit together in silence awaiting the Spirit to move them. The first colony in America governed by "Quakers," met at Rhode Island—laid the foundation of Peace and Arbitration, calling themselves the Society of Friends.

It is necessary to bring one into the atmosphere of the age, because, out of it all, here and there were bubbles forming, struggling up to the Light and Life, with a fervor and zeal that puts us to shame.

A Bit of Background of the Clarke Family

ARNOUL, BISHOP OF METZ IN 641

POWER was in the hands of whoever could head his group, and with as many sons, brothers and relatives of the King's as were in the monasteries, we may imagine they had to enforce strict laws to keep their authority. Metz was a fortified city. The Episcopal See of Alsace Lorraine was on the Moselle. We can picture it in 641, a monastery on a hilltop, surmounted by the Cross, with barbarians not so far off, with its band of holy men withdrawn from the world full of fighting and pillaging, trying to concentrate on the holy life of silence and contemplation, receiving under the authority of its Bishop the men who could not get along in the world.

The Bishop of Metz was called St. Arnoul and he had a son by Doda, called Agsègise, married to Begghe of Landen. He died in 694. He had a son, Pepin of Heristal (a village in Liegois.) He was called "The Forrester" and "The Great." His son was Charles, 689-741 who married Alpaïda. It was this man, Charles Martel or "Hammer," because he struck such blows with his right arm, who checked and drove back the Saracens somewhere between Poitiers and Tours. Before this his title was

Mayor or "Great One of the Palace," and "homme illustre," names which only the kings used in that day.

He had been imprisoned by his father's lawful wife, Plectria, after his father's death. He managed to escape from confinement at Cologne. Once out, he contrived to take the government of all France. His brother Calomen entered a monastery in 747. We would marvel at this if we did not bear in mind the age of wars and soldiery and the veneration for a great leader, left as a heritage to these new Christians from the idolized Roman Emporers down to the present day, when men followed to Death their Generals.

From 716-718 he devasted and conquered the invading Saxons, going as far as Weser. While he was making himself Master at Paris, the Saracens conquered Narbonne. They continued on as far as Bordeaux under their king, Abderame. They pillaged the city. All France was threatened; Christianity hung on the leadership of this Charles. On their fleet horses, with their cruel sabres, nothing seemed able to stop the enemy. There was no Red Cross then! That is a growth of Christianity. Women—except the pretty ones—babies, old persons, the poor and sick were slaughtered; soldiers took as their rightful gain whatever they could get worth having, and way up to the last century the art treasures belonged always to the victor.

Twelve

But Charles was fired by superhuman powers and hacked and slew with his great hammer of an arm, till he met the great Abderame, who finally fell. Without this worthy leader of the Saracens, who also fought for his God—supposed to be the very same Deity, whose Prophet Mohammet had promised all kinds of blessings to those who died fighting for him—the Saracens were easily routed, and in October, 732, Charles broke their army to pieces. "One sees how the Military Powers possess in brief not only the matters of the Churches but even the Monasteries and Abbeys and establish their families there, which often put an end to the holy culture. But if one recalls that the Christian religion without the valour of this Prince would have given place to Mohammedanism, one is more inclined to pardon the unjust and violent means employed to defend and maintain it." (Note: P. 425 Vol. 5, "Art of Verifying dates since Jesus Christ.")

See how Charles Martel placed his family, to show his Christian zeal: Renie was Archbishop of Rouen; Jerome was father of Fulrad, Abbe of St. Denis, Paris; and Bernard was father of Adelard whose son Pepin—who is in our line again—called "Pepin the Short," was ruler with Carlone, of all France, Vieux, Poitiers. He was proclaimed King of the French in the assembly which met at Soissons and was consecrated by St. Boniface, Archbishop of Mayence. Here we see again the power of the Military Leadership to lead men through untold hardships and sufferings and death by their Personality and for a Cause. He conquered the Saxons and ordered them to give him three hundred horses every year, which they somehow evaded doing. He continued to hold back the Saxons and the Saracens, and died in the monastery of St. Denis. The hospitals were started under the church by Holy Men, it is well to remember. It may be interesting to notice that his wife Beretie, or Bertrade, was called "Au grand pied." She was the daughter of Caribert, Comte of Laon, and the mother of Charles and Abbess of Chelles-Gisele. A little touch of color is shown in a story told of Charles Martel's son, Pepin the Short.

While watching a lion fighting a bull, he said to the officers about him, "Who of you has courage enough to go and separate or kill these two animals?" He went himself and killed both animals, saying afterward, "David was little and intimidated Goliath, Alexander was small and surpassed in strength and courage captains much larger in figure than himself." This story and most of these facts are taken from "The Art of Verifying Dates from Jesus Christ."

Strange that while writing of these events of our ancestors the news of baptism of the President of China came over the Radio (Announcer said, "Emperor of China has just been baptized by Episcopal service.")

Think what this means! (Oct. 22, 1930—11:10

p. m.) just as we are about to write of Charlemagne, son of this Pepin the Short.

Charles the Great was consecrated at St. Denis, Paris, 754, by Pope Etienne II. He married Desiderate, afterward returned her to her father and married Hildegarde, descended from Godefroi of the Germans. In 772 he fought and won the Battle of the Torrent, thus subduing the Saxons again, and took the Chateau of Heresborg in Westphalia, and destroyed their temple to Irmensol. They gave him more trouble led by Witikind. In the year 777, the Saxons came from all around to submit to Charles and receive Baptism. Several years later Witikind and Albion received Baptism and became zealous protectors of Christianity. At that time there was more ceremony to a baptism than now. There were catechisms and vigils and fasts and confirmations and sacraments of the Lord's Supper, all connected so that it meant something to live and, in many hundreds and thousands of cases, to die for.

Charlemagne died at seventy-two years of age, after fighting here and there all over France, the Saracens, Saxons, and in 808, the Normans under Godefroi; after ruling France forty-six years and for fourteen years acting as Emperor of Italy, France and Germany. He died at Aix la Chapelle, January 28, 814. In 800, on Christmas day, he was crowned Emperor at Rome. The stone on which he knelt is in St. Peters.

He was crowned in Lombardy with the Iron

Crown. During his fights with the Saracens in Spain his faithful Roland was killed. He besieged Carcassonne and finally Mme. Carcas opened the gates and admitted him and became a Christian. The name of the place is said to come from that time when she held the city by strategy, filling a young pig with all the remaining grain to seem fat, and throwing it over the walls to give the impression that they were well supplied, at the same time sounding the great horn, "Carcas Sonne."

Charlemagne was a Patron of learning and had an Academy in his Palace at Aix la Chapelle; called himself "David" when with his men of letters; spoke Latin and Greek as well as Teutonic, his native tongue. He was very fond of reading and while eating had someone read to him. He established courses in theology and liberal sciences in the Cathedrals and Monasteries. He had baths built and constructed a lighthouse at Bologne.

He is said to have been tall and strong, seven "feet lengths" tall. His head was round. His eyes were large and alert and his nose was large. His countenance was serene and pleasant. He wore a linen shirt, a coat bordered with silk, long trousers, and a cloak. His sword had a gold and silver hilt and belt. He was gentle and kind and worthy of respect. This description is copied from the Encyclopedia Americana.

He traveled from the Pyranees to Germany, from Italy to the Ocean with surprising rapidity.

In the midst of his military expeditions he governed the interior of his kingdom, as if it were peace times. Religion and letters were obligations he could not forget.

In 823 Louis le Debonnaire (so named because of his kindness and his ease in pardoning) assembled a Diet at Nomes.

He endeavored to reform the clergy and make uniformity among the monastic orders under one head, St. Benoit.

In an attempt to reform his court he caused his sisters and nieces to enter convents. His son Lothaire imprisoned him at Aix, then took him to Paris.

Louis was King of France, Germany and Italy. He died in 846. His wife was Judith, daughter of Guelph, Count of Altorf in Swabia. Their son, Charles the Bold, had a daughter Judith who had married Ethelwolph, King of England, and after his death, Baldwin I, Count of Flanders, called "Bras de Fer," meaning "Iron Arm." This is our first glimpse of England. Judith must have lived there while Ethelwolph lived, so it is not so strange to find her son Baldwin II, Count of Flanders called "The Bold," married to Alfretha the daughter of Alfred the Great, King of England, around 900. Boldwin II died in 918.

Flanders being near England, it is not strange that much interest was shown in that direction. Our line is continued through Arnolph I, "The Great,"

Count of Flanders, to Baldwin III who married Maud, daughter of J. Herman Billung, Duke of Saxony; all Christians now for centuries; through Arnolph II, Count of Flanders, who married Susanna, daughter of Berenger II, King of Italy; through Baldwin IV, Count of Flanders and Artois, called "Fair Beard," who died in 1034, whose wife was Ogive, daughter of Frederick I, Count of Bavaria and Luxembourg.

Their son was Baldwin V, Count of Flanders, "The Pious," who died in 1067. His wife was Adele, daughter of Robert II, King of France, and widow of Richard III, Duke of Normandy. Their daughter, Maud (or Matilda) married in 1053 William, Duke of Normandy, called "The Conqueror," born in 1024, who conquered the English at the Battle of Hastings and as King of England in 1066, brought so strong a Norman-French influence into that country that French was spoken and taught for three hundred years.

They had a son born at Selby in Yorkshire in 1070 —died 1135—who became Henry I, King of England. His wife was Matilda, daughter of Malcolm Canmore III, King of Scotland, by Queen Margaret, sister and heiress of Edgar Atheling. Their daughter Maud, widow of Henry IV, Emperor of Germany, was born in 1104 and died on September 10, 1167; married 1127 Geoffrey Plantagenet, born 1111, died 1150, son of Faulk, Count of Anjou and Ermengard.

Their son Henry II, King of England, born 1133, died 1189, married Eleanor of Aquitaine, by this marriage, the kings of England claimed large parts of France, Aquitaine and Guienne, through Eleanor's father, William V, Duke of Guienne and Aquitaine.

Now their son John, King of England, 1160-1216, married, in 1200, Isabelle, daughter of Aymer Taillefer, Earl of Angouleme, another strong tie to parts of France for the kings of England to claim.

Their son, Henry III, King of England, 1206-1272, married Eleanor, daughter of Berenger, Count of Provence and Beatrice of Savoy—more French Alliance. Edward I, King of England, 1239-1307, married Eleanor, daughter of Ferdinand III, King of Castile and Leon.

Edward I and Eleanor had a daughter Joan born at Acre, who married Gilbert, Earl of Gloucester.

They had a daughter, Elizabeth de Claré, who married Theobold—Baron Verdon—whose daughter, Isabel de Verdon, married Henry de Ferrers, Baron of Groby; his son was

Henry
his son William
his son Thomas
his son Henry
his daughter Elizabeth, who married James Clark
 their son George
  his son James
  his son William
  his son Jeremy Clarke

This is only written to show what blood came to Rhode Island, and be sure, if it was too blue, the fresh salt breezes and sea-air of Newport, fairest City in America, surely supplied the necessary red corpuscles!

MAP

W E
S

NEW FRANCE

ATLANTIC OCEAN

NEW ENGLAND

JEREMY CLARK
FRANCIS LATHAM DURBIN

EDWARD I
1231

DAU
ELEANOR

NEWPORT
JEREMY CLARK, PRESIDENT
OF RHODE ISLAND COLONY
1678

FERDINAND III
KING OF CASTILE AND LEON

MARRIED
KING OF NAVARRE
MARRIED
ELVIRA
DAU OF

EL CID
1040 109

THE ALMORABI
DEFEATED BY
EL CID

THIS MAP
ENDEAVORS TO INDICATE
THE CONFLICT TO DEFEND
CHRISTIANITY
IN EUROPE - ALSO
THE
REMARKABLE ANCESTRY
OF
JEREMY CLARK
PRESIDENT OF
RHODE ISLAND COLONY 1678

NORTH SEA

FLANDERS

MEDITERRANEAN SEA

MOSCOW

ALPHTHA 813
DAU OF ALFRED FM L MAI
MARRIED
BALDWIN 30

ÆTHELWULF
OF KENT

HENRIE
MARRIED
ELEANOR DAU
DUKE OF AQUITAINE

BALDWIN I 862
MARRIED
JUDITH
GR GRAND DAUGHTER
OF CHARLEMAGNE

DAU KING
OF GERMANY

CHARLEMAGNE
CONVERTS SAXONS 779
AT BRESS AND WET IT IN INO

GOIN
OF TO
BLACK
SEA

VLADIMIR OF
KIEV

MA PRINE OF KIEV

MD ADELAIDE

CHARLES MARTEL
DEFEATS SARACENS 732

CLOVIS DEFEATS VISIGOTHS
IN 507
MARRIED CLOTILDA
OF BURGUNDY

CHARLEMAGNE
MARRIED
HILDEGARDE OF
SWABIA

ARNOLPH
OF
FLANDERS

SUSANNA
DAU OF
BERENGER II
ITALY

CHARLEMAGNE
CROWNED EMPEROR
OF
WESTERN EUROPE
AT ROME
800

BASED ON
"ANCESTRY OF
JEREMY CLARK"
BY A.R. JUSTICE
AND
THE
PLANTAGENETT ANCESTRY
BY
W.H. TURTON

DRAWN BY
ROD LJOHN JR

PART TWO

*Being the Story of the First Settle-
ment in America of the Society of
Friends, Who discounted War and
Actually Attempted a Kingdom of
Peace*

England 1609

"A-hunting we will go; a-hunting we will go!"

SO started the great sport of the day. What a
snapping of whips, a barking of dogs and general confusion there was, this cold, windy day of
February! The orders of the hunt were heard.

Such a chorus of shouts and flying heels, as the
various servants of the Royal Sovereign, King
James of Scotland, England, Wales and France,
hastened to do his bidding! They were to hunt
with falcons; the young princes were to venture
forth. Straight and handsome, Prince Henry was
mounted on his favorite horse, with Prince Charlie
beside him, attended by the Special Falconer, Lewis
Latham. The brown-feathered bird, blind-folded,
sat clutching Prince Henry's left gloved wrist.
Latham carried a falcon himself, and his attendant a cage with several more of the birds. This
cage was strapped onto the fellow's shoulders.
With a winding of horns, and some ceremony, the
party left the courtyards and rode off at a good
speed for the moors.

"My faith, it's a glorious day! Never would one
think it mid-winter, Latham, I never saw you so
gay; is it but the cold air and sunny skies, or hast
good news, my man?" asked Henry, always kind
and sympathetic to his fellows.

LEWIS LATHAM, FALCONER TO PRINCES HENRY AND CHARLES

Twenty-four

"My Prince, it's indeed a happy day, for have I not the cutest morsel of a baby girl sleeping like a rosebud beside her mother! She is to be christened tomorrow 'Frances,' and may she serve her country bravely, being free to breathe this air."

"Best luck be with the babe, and with you all! My first quarry shall be for the mother. You shall take it with my greetings." Thus Henry showed his kind heart.

On they rode till the open moor stretched around them on all sides. Rocks, brush, and gorse, where the grouse and the rabbits loved to live, showed the hunters where to halt. The hood was removed from Prince Henry's falcon and the bird released from her leash. She flew about her master's head, while the horses stood with ears alert and eyes intent. At the signal, away off and up flew the fine bird, with outspread wings high above. She could, with those piercing eyes, detect the soft brown rabbit or the grouse, hidden to the riders, — so the eye of the destroyer can observe, all unobserved, his victim. Then, gliding down to a lower plane, in a circle about her prey, she darted, swift as an arrow from the tightly drawn bow, directly for the back of the soft furry rabbit and grasped it in her talons. Beating her wings to return to the air, she flew back to her prince and master with the prize. Henry took the still warm creature by its long ears and, holding it high, with a smile handed it to Latham for his wife.

Alas, that the promising young Prince Henry, beloved by his people, was to die three years later after a lingering illness! His father refused to have mourning for him. Had he lived, the Revolution might have been spared, for he was of an opposite nature to his brother Charlie, who was soft, fond of luxury and flattery, and was extravagant. He loved his lap-dogs, his long perfumed hair—was not in touch with the ills and dangers of his country. Never having to fight, he became a moral as well as a physical coward.

Lewis Latham and His Daughter

LATHAM continued to train and supervise the hawks used by the Prince. At this time hawking was one of the favorite sports of royalty, and the falcons were specially used by the royal sovereigns. Latham was Sergeant of the hawks in 1627, under Charles I. His out-door life gave him such vigor that he lived to be one hundred years old.

During this time his little daughter developed and unfolded from childhood to womanhood. She was most pleasant to look at, with her fine figure, soft brown hair blowing over her shoulders, ruddy cheeks and white brow, her eyes shining with cheer and good health. You may be sure her father told her all he knew of the tradition of falconry; how it was a favorite sport 2000 B. C. in China; how the Egyptians were also fond of it, and the Persians; how the Crusaders brought the love of the sport to England, and, even before that, William the Conqueror held it for his favorite pastime.

Surely he taught her how to tame the young females by bandaging the eyes to feed them, so as to accustom them to human hands, and even to teach them to train their own young. The little Frances must have watched the birds plume their feathers, and sealed their eyes and aided at "imping" or mending their broken feathers, helped put on their hoods and jesses or bands of leather on their legs, to which rings with bells were hung, and also leather leashes to hold them by. She herself must have run with her father over the moors when the hawks needed exercise, and had some practice in training new hawks. Latham would tell her stories on such occasions.

"Did you ever hear of El Cid and his lion? That's a tale for you," said Latham.

"Tell me about it; do, please, father."

"Well, the Cid had a pet lion. He gloried in being brave, and because the lion was the strongest and fiercest animal, he made a pet of the creature. El Cid had two daughters whom he arranged to marry to two young men named Gonzales, of good birth, but who were suspected of being cowards. So, one day, while the Cid was napping — or pretending to nap — and the rest of his attendants, including the Gonzales brothers, were lingering after their hearty repast, the lion broke loose — or perhaps it was all done purposely. Such a commotion as the suitors made, showing by their terror that their one thought was to save their own skins, and in a most cowardly way. The lion being a pet, of course the young men were in no danger, but, rather, were the laughing stock of the others. You can never imagine how boiling was their hot Spanish blood with hidden rage and vengeance until I tell you that they wreaked their spite on the Cid's daughters by marrying them and starting with them for their homes far away. And when they came to a thick forest, they beat the two daughters of the Cid, taking their clothes from them and leaving them for the wild beasts to destroy. Fortunately, the girls were found by one of the Cid's loyal followers, who took them back. After a time they were married to the sons of the King of Navarre.

"Man was given power in the Garden of Eden to tame the wild beasts and use them for his needs. This great gyrfalcon I am training, as you know, is the kind used only by kings, and is a regal bird indeed."

Her childhood passed. In this healthy clean air, which gave her a robust body and a clear mind, and in companionship with her father, Frances grew to womanhood.

London—"The Plague"

A FEW years before, in 1603, a horrible plague had carried off 1,000,000 people in Egypt. But not till 1625 did it reach London. At that time, the city was at a low point as regards health conditions; the streets were narrow and paved, the second story of the houses projected some feet over the lower, and the third story still some feet over the second, so that sunshine could barely do any disinfecting. Street lamps were few and far between, the lamp-lighters and watchmen often getting weary and dropping into the ale-houses for a glass of refreshment and a bit of gossip. The housewives, having no pipes to carry off the filthy water, emptied it into the streets from the handiest window. All this in foggy weather, with many beggars and drunkards, made nights in the poorer quarters of London something hideous. Somehow, the plague started, and 35,000 died amid awful scenes. Added to this terrible condition were heard the groaning of the sick, the weeping of the stricken families and then the ominous stillness as the death wagon would drive to the door to take the corpse, with hundreds of others, to be thrown into the pit in the common burying ground for the plague victims — for many years after a place to be shunned. No doubt, many died of fright and many were buried alive before they breathed their last.

WILLIAM DUNGAN'S PERFUME SHOP — LONDON
1636

Thirty-two

It is no wonder that persons of aesthetic tastes and delicate noses should have liked perfume, strong and noticeable. Hence we find William Dungan, Gentleman Perfumer, in London. Perfume could be made from musk ox, also from ambre-gris from whales. Whaling was a paying industry in New England on account of the demand for the bones, oil and ambre-gris. The English were active in this business, the Muscovey Company being formed for that purpose. We may picture the long curly-wigged dandies of the Court of Charles I sniffing at the various vials of odours which would be dashed over their curls and soaked on the center of their handkerchiefs which they could hold over their noses when necessary, so that they might not have to smell the odorous streets of London. The perfumes, so common today, were originated to overcome some of the most offensive conditions on record.

To such a sharply contrasted atmosphere came Frances Latham. She had married William Dungan, Gentleman, said to be descended through the Dungans of Dublin from Edward III, King of England. They lived in the Parish of St. Martin's in the Fields, Middlesex.

By the time Frances was twenty-five, Mr. Dungan had died, leaving her a widow, with a little daughter Barbara, a son William, another daughter Frances and a son Thomas. They were left ten pounds apiece by their father. The plague had attacked Milan in 1630, and in Holland in 1635-7 it was raging. Probably through rats in the ships or rags of some wretched beggar, it broke out again in London this year, the year Mr. Dungan died.

At that time the young widow paid taxes and the next year was assessed thirteen shillings on account of "the long continuance of the plague." This tax was levied by the wardens of the church for the relief and maintenance of the poor.

Frances was living at Covent Garden on the east side of Bedford Street. How she must have longed for the clean air and sunshine of her father's home, and to get away from London with those little children, to make them strong and useful men and women. How could she do it herself in the midst of such surroundings and crowds of paupers by the thousands in rags and filth, snatching at bones and crusts like hungry wolves? There were probably a million beggars and paupers in England at this time.* Human like herself — and she could do so little.

---

*"Out of a population of five million, 1,330,000 were paupers and beggars in 1696.

Jeremy Clarke

A T this time the Lord Treasurer of England was
Richard Weston, Earl of Portland, who had a
sister, Mary, married to William Clarke, gentleman. Jeremy Clarke, their son, was well connected.
His great-grandfather was son of Elizabeth
Ferrers, who claimed descent from the daughter of
Edward I, Joanna of Acre, where she was born
when her mother Eleanor of Castile accompanied
her husband on his crusade.

Like many youths full of the spirit of adventure,
and seeing little chance at home to rise to his full
stature, Jeremy Clarke deliberated over the idea
of crossing to that new and promising land, England was encouraging her brave sons to colonize.
The tutor of Prince Henry had been Sir William
Alexander of Scotland. He established a colony
to found a New Scotland, led by his own son, in the
New World. The King, approving, granted him a
large tract of land, north of the Kennebec River to
the St. Lawrence, including the peninsula. This'
was named Nova Scotia, and to insure its success,
a number of prominent Scotchmen were induced to
support the undertaking by furnishing, each, six
men to actually colonize the country, and a large
sum of money to pay the expenses of the undertaking. In return, the King granted them six miles

of land along the waterways and the title of Baron, to be perpetual. This idea was the same as that which William the Conquerer used to induce men of brawn and substance to settle in England at the time of his invasion. The names of the men who joined together for this promising venture are outstanding names in history. These grants and sales continued in the 18th century, sometimes causing much trouble.

Alexander had chosen from among the gentry such great patriots as Sir Robert Gordon Knight, Sir Duncan Campbell, Sir John Weynes, Sir William Douglas, Sir Donald MacDonald, Sir Alexander Gordon, David Livington, William Earl Marshall, Alexander Strachan, Robert Lewis, Richard Murray, John Colcuhourn, John Leslie, James Gordon, Gilbert Ramsay, Thomas Nicholson of Carnock, John Nicolson of Leswade and other men of vision and venture. Had Prince Henry lived this might have made a different turn to the struggles of New England. But, alas, the Revolution under the weak and extravagant reign of Charles I affected tragically the Scotch settlement. The supplies cut off, harassed by the French, they were neglected and starved out. Some of the survivors straggled down the coast of Maine under the protection of Massachusetts, others welcomed the French when under Charles the Second, the fort was ordered demolished and it became a French colony.

The reports of the settlement at Nova Scotia were discouraging. At this time, 1637-8, Fort Royal was practically given over to the French.

So it would be better to go to New England. Like every brave colonizer, Jeremy Clarke sought to choose a suitable person who would be able to rear him children. He found a ready and courageous spirit to share the hardship and comfort his hearth. In 1637, he married Frances Latham Dungan, bravely fathering the four little Dungan children, and together they set forth for the New Colony at Rhode Island.

One day, before sailing, as she walked by Charing Cross with her little Barbara, the child questioned her about the wording on the cross. Frances told her the story of Edward I and his love for his Spanish wife. Edward was only a youth of fifteen when his mother, Eleanor of Provence, wife of Henry III, King of England, escorted him to Bordeaux and across the Pyrenees to Burgos and betrothed him to the charming little daughter of Ferdinand III, King of Leon. This little girl of scarcely ten years, named Eleanor, a short time later came to damp, cold England, with her retinue of servants, riding on donkeys and mules, much to the gaping astonishment of the Londoners. She brought heavy carpets and tapestries to cover the cold floors and stone walls of her rooms. When Edward, many years later, went on his crusade, Eleanor insisted on accompanying him, against all advice and threats. At Acre in Syria a little daughter was born, named Joanna. On this pilgrimage the life of Edward was many times in danger. Once an attempt was nearly successful when, as he lay ill, an assassin entered the room and threw a poisoned dagger at him. He warded it off with his arm, receiving the wound which nearly cost him his life. He was ever after grateful for Eleanor's unfailing care and devotion at this time, when she is said to have, with her own lips, sucked the poison from the wound.

Later, his enemies in Scotland required him to invade that country. He caught and caused to be killed William Wallace. At the same time Eleanor was very ill in England. Before he could return, she died, in the home of a gentleman named Weston, we are told, at the early age of forty-six. Heart-broken, Edward had crosses erected at each place where the funeral procession rested on its long journey from Grantham to London. Thirteen of these crosses were built, among the number those at Northampton, Dunstable and Waltham; and the last was at Charing Cross — some say named for "Chère Reine," Eleanor. These crosses make resting places for all weary travellers. Here the poor heard many preachers, and food was distributed to them.

The New Experiment

I T is important to have in mind the very different
motives that urged the men and women to come
to New England. In our own day, when new countries are opened, there are some who brave the wilds
for commercial reasons, some for their health, some
for the mere love of exploring and overcoming
dangers, some to enlighten the ignorant natives, and
others are encouraged to try another atmosphere,
owing to their failure to get along at home. These
last—the restless souls, out of joint with the world
— are misfits of society.

So it was in New England. Led by the English
trades, and guided by men of vision in England,
accompanied by conservative men to govern and
direct them, they were an unknown quality, as
regards character, to try out this new experiment.
They were men and women, high strung, opinion-
ated, ready to suffer for what they believed — not
always to suffer in silence, however — men and
women who, when the Catholic religion was at
stake and the casket which contained the Sacred
Truths was smashed, eagerly, like hungry souls,
grasped parts of the Whole Great Truth. We cannot call these men and women leaders of philosophy, but in a certain way they presented certain
schools of thought, with their own personal inter-

pretation. In England these factions, the Brown-
ists, Anabaptists, Calvinists, became split again
according to their teachers' ideas which often went
through strange phases of religious zeal when trans-
planted across the Atlantic. So we find the popular
young preacher of Salem proclaiming a few new
revolutionary ideas, — Roger Williams, adored by
many, actually menacing the throne of England's
right to occupy land by right of discovery; a new
doctrine making illegal all right to territory unless
paid for. Another point, creating consternation
among the Clergy of the New England, was that
Roger claimed no right to the fruit of labor in the
fields from his flock; holding strong views, spoken
and written with unmistakable contempt for the
clergy who did not earn their own living. In this
point he was also inflexible. We may imagine the
shock and surprise at this violent attack. It must
have been more peaceful to a man of Roger Williams' energetic type to go out and dig in his garden
than to listen to the woes of the homesick, troubled,
confused congregation. But this has not been found
practical for clergy any more than for lawyers or
physicians or men in public service generally.
Something is due them to allow them to be free
from destitution, at least, if they are to be called
upon night and day for the spiritual needs of their
flock. They must have some time to prepare the
all important sermons, and be well-read on all
points of doctrine and philosophy. Perhaps never

in the history of the world has there met together
in a wilderness surrounded by Indians and wolves
such a learned group of men and women, some of
them penetrating depths and heights of thought
unequalled since the days of the martyrs in Rome,
filled with that same desire to suffer for the Truth,
but, alas, lacking in charity; for "Charity covers a
multitude of sins." . . . "Charity suffers long and
is kind." And at least all agree that sins were never
covered or condoned in New England; the stocks,
the whipping post, the hangman and banishment
gave every publicity possible to offenders.

The Exodus

WILLIAM CODDINGTON, former treasurer and
assistant òf the Massachusetts Bay Colony,
was acquainted with the Marburys. They all came
from Boston, old St. Butolf's Town, in Lincoln-
shire. He had heard Anne Marbury Hutchinson,
daughter of Reverend Francis Marbury of London,
discourse. Her mother was the sister of Sir Erasmus
Dryden, grandfather of John Dryden, the poet.
Her husband William Hutchinson was devoted to
her. He was a man of mild, pleasant disposition,
and like the other men and women was more than
impressed with her fire and zeal which made her
an eloquent speaker.

The contrast between the rigid, proper observ-
ance of the letter of the law, on one side, and the
lightning and thunder effects of the discourses of
the separating preachers, produced an effect of evi-
dent destruction to the minds of the men in charge
of the new colony. Certain men, among whom were
Sir Christopher Gardiner and Sir Harry Vane, even
made complaint of the intolerance of these governors. They certainly had their problems. It must
have been with a certain relief that Coddington
undertook to lead the group of agitators out of
Massachusetts, after publicly defending the persecuted Anne Hutchinson at her trial, much to the

regret of Governor Winthrop, always his friend. He was one of the few men with charity enough to stand by her in her darkest hour.

That they were no ordinary men and women is proved by their future record. Led by the Spirit, these few persons set forth.

Roger Williams had escaped the wrath of his opponents and, after a cruel winter in hiding with the "filthy Indians," emerged at last with an enduring friendship for these savages who had sheltered him. He brought out material for his famous "Key to the Indian Language" and with his small band of exiles who had joined him at Rehoboth, he crossed the Seekonk and settled around the Spring on the West side of the opposite peninsula, naming it Providence. The next year a group of men and women followed his trail to Providence in what is now the State of Rhode Island. They were associated with the fanatical sect of Anabaptists. This sect originated in Munster where John Leyden in 1535, was the leader of a group of fanatics, who, however high their motives, were advertised by their acts of superstition and debauchery. John Fox, another religious leader, exerting a powerful influence through his "Book of Martyrs," was responsible for many of the eccentricities, we might say, which made prominent this little group of New England.

Surely Anne Marbury, wife of William Hutchinson, held a truly remarkable influence over the Clergy of Boston. She is the first English woman we know of who held meetings in the new world. When she had assembled her group, she would declaim to them, ridiculing the words and gestures of some of the Boston pastors. She certainly exerted a great spell over Sir Harry Vane, the beautiful young Governor of Massachusetts, William Coddington, the Assistant, and William Dyer, whose wife was her devoted shadow and, like many others, perhaps lost her head, if not her heart. But one thing she forgot: if a woman wishes to be a spiritual leader, she must be above reproach. No one can read the account of her from Winthrop's careful diary and not wonder somewhat about her. It was not the custom for a woman to collect men, and especially to allow them to be driven out of their respectable positions in affairs, because they were chivalrous enough to stand up for the defense of a prosecuted woman.

Coddington was a colonist and at his home outside Boston, around his fireplace, a group of men and women discussed their plans for the future. As soon as the adherents of Anne Hutchinson were requested to leave Massachusetts, they "thought to go to the Dutch" on Long Island.

The first step was to Roger Williams' settlement. This company of men, women, children, cows, pigs and horses trailed through the woods to his door, to halt, before passing over to Long Island where Mrs. Hutchinson was eager to go and be under the tolerant Dutch rule.

Beside Roger Williams' rude house was the home of Richard Scott and his wife Hannah Marbury, who was Anne's sister.

Roger had something to suggest which, after careful consideration, met with hearty approval. He urged them to remain under English rule. Owing to his friendly relations with the Indian Chief Conanicus, he arranged for the purchase of a beautiful Island where they would have a chance to show what an ideal place could be developed from Christian principles.

He evidently did not want Quakers in Providence, nor did they care to be under his leadership. Though next-door neighbors, the views of the Scotts and Williams never accorded, and were always a thorn in the flesh to Roger.

The Quakers were imbued with Anabaptism and the philosophy and small, rather stubborn, points of John Fox. They would not remove their hats, a sign that they bowed to no one but Jesus Christ, their one great leader. Also they used "thee" and "thou," familiar terms to all, regardless of position, to signify equality of man. Also they refused to swear by heaven or by earth, holding "Yea" and "Nay" sufficient, as they were disciples of Truth.

Roger Williams took Coddington to negotiate with the old Chief Conanicus.

The silent old king sat impressive with his black smoky-filmed eyes gleaming at Coddington. Dressed in the modest substantial suit with knickers and heavy wool stockings, with a smiling ruddy face beneath a broad-brimmed felt hat, Mr. Coddington drew the respect and approval of the old man. He represented the group, as he later declared. Roger Williams, after a year of hard work in establishing his home and garden, was tanned and hardened, but kind.

Money meant nothing to Indians. Nothing pleased them more than red coats with brass buttons shining in the gloomy smoky atmosphere of their wigwams. Hoes meant for them food—warmth and food, the things most necessary to sustain life through the chill, cold winters and damp days. So, for what seems to us nothing much, but which cost dearly to the settlers of their own supplies, the island of Aquidnick was purchased for coats and hoes.

The company of men and women were light-hearted as they travelled over the trail and crossed the narrowest part of the Tiverton River by boat, to the northern point of Rhode Island or Aquidnick. Here the pasturage was promising and they made their first settlement, calling it Portsmouth.

An Ideal State: Rhode Island

THERE is no doubt that many became slightly, if not seriously, unbalanced owing to the hardships and continual religious wrangles. With the Bible—the English version of James I being the most cherished possession of these men and women —and with the doors thrown open to the public to come in and feast on this formerly rare book, came the knaves and gluttons and pigs and fools. At one time shortly before this, the bars and taverns were so noisy and such lewd jokes and conversation from the Holy Book were made that stringent laws had to be passed about publishing it. Only licensed printers in London and elsewhere were permitted to print it. William Alexander, the colonizer of Nova Scotia, had finished King James I translation of the Psalms and after the King's death Charles I tried to force his father's version on the Scotch. Which was not a popular move.

This island colony was not undertaken without great forethought. Founded on the ancient plan of the Hebrews before Saul became King, they decided after studying their treasured Bible that history had proved the wise old Priest Samuel to be correct. They found that under the rule of judges Peace had reigned in the Hebrew Kingdom, and that Samuel's prophesy of wars and troubles following the election of a king had been realized. Their King was Jesus Christ, the all-powerful but unseen Ruler of the Universe. They chose, therefore, from among their number, the man who had best shown his ability to judge wisely and well. It was a sacred honor which they gave to William Coddington. With their hearts and minds they hoped to build a colony to be a model for the people of the New England.

As more persons joined them, and complications arose, discussions and criticism appeared. In April 28, 1639, Mrs. Hutchinson's husband was chosen judge at Portsmouth. Coddington and his supporters removed to the further end of the island in May, 1638-9, building huts at first. This left thirty-one persons in Portsmouth, among them Samuel Gorton, John Wickes, Sampson Sholton, Robert Potter. Fifteen of the men could not sign their names.

On the other end of the island there was a beautiful harbor, a great chance for trading and commerce. Nicholas Easton and his two sons, Peter and John, had built the first house where now stands the Naval Training Station. In all, there were about two hundred English on the whole island by 1639 —twice as many as in Providence. The first winter one hundred and eight bushels of corn were divided among ninety-six persons; so the population increased in spite of the isolation of the island. There was a Dutch trading post nearer by water than

Boston; so many times the islanders were grateful for supplies from the Dutch, especially when Massachusetts Colony could not spare any of these needs at the time.

There was great excitement when the Indians chased the wolves off the Island. No hunt in Old England could compare with it. Roger Williams arranged with Mantinomi at the opening of the settlement to have them remove the wolves, always a nightmare to settlers. To live in a log cabin, to hear the wind howl and moan through the long cold winter night, to know that the good man of the house was not yet back from some distant settlement—then to hear that sound never to be forgotten: the howls of a pack of wolves, starving, hungry for flesh—were some of the early horrors which the Island was soon to be relieved of. The people at first had no fire-arms, as the Quakers did not believe it right.

The Newport colony extended five miles east and north over the southern half of the island of Aquidnick or Rhode Island. John Clarke, lately came from Massachusetts Bay Colony, was a man much respected by Governor Winthrop. He was a physician of excellent qualities. With Nicholas Easton he was requested to inform Sir Harry Vane by writing about the new colony at Newport, and to ask him to try to procure a Patent of the Island from His Majesty Charles I. The title of judge was soon changed to the regulation title of Governor, used in general among the English colonies. William Coddington was elected Governor with William Brenton as Deputy Governor. Nicholas Easton, John Coggeshall, William Hutchinson and John Porter were made Assistants. As Hutchinson, Brenton, and Porter were then living in Portsmouth, this plan united the colony again. Robert Jeffreys of Newport was one treasurer, William Baulston of Portsmouth the other. Almost from the start Frances became vitally interested in the affairs of the colony of Newport, as the Constables for the whole island were Jeremy Clarke of Newport and John Sanford of Portsmouth, while Henry Bull of Newport was made Sergeant of the Island. All were men of education and high qualities, and later at least half of them rose to the head of the government in Rhode Island.

The Clarkes' First Appearance
in Newport

IT was rather an important part which awaited
Frances and her young husband. Jeremy Clarke
was present at the first meeting when on March
16, 1638, a group of men began the business of
the new settlement and called it Newport. William
Coddington was again appointed Judge, Nicholas
Easton, John Coggeshall, William Brenton, John
Clarke, Jeremy Clarke, then thirty-two years old,
Thomas Hazard and Henry Bull were appointed
elders with William Dyer as Secretary. Jeremy
Clarke was thus a supporter of Mr. Coddington
from the beginning of the Colony. This must have
been very pleasing to Mrs. Clarke for she was indeed proud of her husband's modest yet confident
bearing. This year a son was born to the Clarkes.
He was named Walter. Little he knew of the hard
life his family was enduring for his future comfort.

With the inspiring presence of Dr. John Clarke
added to the colony, Frances felt no especial fear
in beginning this baby boy's life on such a pleasant
Island as Aquidnick. Where could one see lovelier
sunsets than on the west shore, looking across to
the long tree-covered Island of Conanicut. All the
bay would be rosy and silver with little dancing
waves when the breezes would blow. Now and then

canoes with friendly Narragansett Indians would pass by; once in a long while a trade ship would drop anchor. Mr. Coddington having lived in England and in Boston where the sheep markets were famous, became naturally interested in sheep-raising. Mr. Easton with his young sons undertook tanning of hides. Mr. Dyer undertook the task of making hats of leather or felt. Other busied themselves with hewing lumber and making cement from oyster shells and clam shells. This last was a much complained of occupation as the smell of burning shells was not at all pleasant. Lime was found in the north of the settlement of Providence, a little later.

Frances was always busy in her home or with her children. They must be taught letters and numbers, each had little tasks, one could sit with the baby while one could help with the garden. Little children were as serious as their elders. Nothing makes a two-year-old little boy and girl happier than to play they are keeping house or helping mother. With patience as a constant companion, every mother knows the many steps these little busy feet save her, if kindly and happily directed.

But no fine little boy or girl will take bossing or rude commands from anyone, even of the highest authority, without conflict. It is rather a craven-spirited child who has to be bullied to obey.

Herodias Long

To introduce this girl we must return to dark, damp, smoky, fog-choked London of 1636. Narrow streets, reeking gutters, forms coming into the lamplight and fading quickly into the gloom. Old St. Paul's, with its large black shape overshadowing the market place where horses, swine, cattle, fowls, and hungry beggars, thieves and wretches slunk about in the shadows.

Here one might have truly seen a tall adventurer, John Hicks, leading by the hand a young girl of thirteen who was quietly sobbing.

"Cheer up, will you, child! Am I not to make you my bride this evening! Are we not to sail away from this gloomy town, across the silver-gold seas to America where you will be free! Come now, smile a bit and stop moping!"

The girl threw up her head and showed a bright gleaming smile, beneath the lamp, as she tightened her grip on his hand. And something of the look of the martyrs came to her face. If she had known all the suffering before her, she couldn't have endured the thought of it.

"You are good to me, John. Since father died, I have had a dreadful existence, with the thought that my mother could no longer support her children. You are saving me from the taverns, John, and I will try to be a good wife to you!"

They descended the steps to the little church of St. Faiths, below St. Paul's, where the priest was very happy to marry them. There was so much misery in London, so many women, old and wretched, though in years hardly much older than thirty, that when a pretty young girl came to be married, with a strong, able-bodied young man, she, at least, had a chance.

"We purpose to go to America to seek our fortunes."

"May God be with you, and help you to establish a new and a better world overseas!" prayed the priest.

Herodias Long, the young girl, was built of steel, or she could not have lived through it all. Tall and slight, with straight cropped brown hair, a face pale with large blue eyes, a rather large mouth and strong hands.

Hicks was on his way to America, and realizing that any country without a woman to cook and sew and work for him would be unbearable, had made up his mind that Herodias would do very well, as he knew her friends who were allowing her to live with them after her father's death. They were pleased that Hicks should escort her to church, and perhaps relieved to have her off their hands. When the young adventurers returned, and Herodias told her friends that she had that evening married John

Hicks, they were perhaps somewhat anxious as to the manner in which Herodias' mother would receive the news.

Two days later, John Hicks burst into the room where Herodias was sitting, and said, "All aboard, Herod! The ship sails down the Thames at sundown. Tie up your belongings and come along to the Land of Indians and Happiness! I can make a fortune for you there, so that when you get to be a grown lady you shall wear jewels and silks!"

They soon were ready. The few belongings of Herodias, which her mother had sent to her on hearing of her marriage, were tied up in a woolen shawl. They were four silver spoons, some fine linen for caps, some gray silk and a bag of silver which she had carefully hidden in the wood-box as being the last place a thief would look.

"I have bought a sheep and a cow, Herodias, for we shall find a little home as soon as we get to Boston. I expect to get many skins from the Indians outside the town. Here is a little hand spinning-wheel I bought, for you will have to make many stockings. They say the winters are cold and the snow sometimes three or four feet deep there! Come, girl, the time and tide wait for no one."

Herodias was eager for the great adventure. John Hicks was full of good spirits and hopeful with excitement.

On their way to the ship, at Fleet Street, they passed a book shop and stopped to see what the crowd was looking at. It proved to be a new book printed by Gregory Dexter, a master-printer. John bought a copy, thinking he might find the book useful if he was to have dealings with the Indians. As they passed London Bridge, Herodias looked with horror on the heads of the wretches, which were rotting on the tall spikes as a frightful warning to traitors!

On the ship they met some kindly persons, but mostly adventurers like themselves who were going across to take the great chance rather than face the dreadful conditions in England. Confusion of mind, body and estate, caused by the opening of men's minds! Before printing, there was so little light let in on the minds of the people; but now the doors were open and they didn't know how to use all that they saw!

Hicks went to Weymouth where he and his young wife lived for over two years. What hard nerve and body testing days and nights for the young girl! They became more and more interested in the society of Friends; nevertheless, they had a kindly feeling toward the Dutch, for they were the ones who had the best swords and guns. Holland gin also played an important role in the early colonial days. After the completely exhausted condition which the cold and more often the wet had produced, a good drink of gin would warm the human frame from tip to toe and start the tired heart pumping again. They followed Ann Hutchinson to Rhode Island very soon.

It was shearing time, and Coddington's sheep were being turned from balls of wool to timid, ashamed looking, bleating creatures who ran about looking for a place to hide! Everyone had to help at the wool washing and carding. Then such days of spinning, such evenings of knitting. No decent woman was without her wool-work, for it meant life itself for the coming winter.

In Massachusetts the Quakers were forbidden to meet and were greatly persecuted. Young Mrs. Hicks had become interested in their sect and her husband decided that Newport would be a safer place to live in, away from the Massachusetts authorities. Herodias lived by the spirit; it was a real presence to her. Like many persons condemned to hard and uncongenial tasks, her thoughts were much too luminous and large to be confined in a little ten-by-twenty cabin of a house.

One evening, after Hicks had returned from his work, rather worn, and had taken his tumbler of gin, and as they sat at the plain little supper of pork and cornbread which Herodias had prepared, Hicks began:

"Herodias, I'll be cursed if you shall go on with this crowd here! I could do much better for you with the Dutch. Let us go to New Amsterdam!"

"John," replied Herodias, "you do not know what you are asking! My mother and brothers are now in Her Majesty's service. Do you think I could forsake my country and go to live with the

Dutch! They tell me they are half drunk most of the time!"

"What do you mean?" shouted Hicks. "That you refuse to come with me! For I have decided to join them. My fighting blood is up, and I think they will get this whole country from the English. 'Tis theirs for first settling and trading, anyway you look at it, girl! I left England for my fortune, and now am here in their colonies; and look how they treat their own countrymen. Cut off their ears, slit their tongues, stick them in pillories if a man so much as kiss his wife on Sunday! I tell you I am going, and you are coming, too, do you hear me?"

He rose angrily as Herodias stood up, with her head high, and blazing eyes, and said to him:

"John Hicks, when I was in great sorrow you took me to wife and brought me to this rough world. I loved you for your kindness. But I love my own soul, and no one, not even my husband, shall tell me that my faith is as nothing, to be turned over like a page in your book, with new words for every day of the week! When my brothers are fighting for England, think you I would go to the Dutch? I cannot stop you; but go with you, I will not! Here is a great opportunity for us—take it and be industrious. I know I am young and stupid in the ways of the world, but here there are kind people who will help me to weave and make warm clothes and teach me to cook the strange fruits for winter food."

"You dare to talk so to me! Very well, ungrateful girl, I am going without you, and what's more, I shall never come back. Do you hear that? You may beg or starve for all of me! I am through with trailing you about." And seizing his cloak, he wrapped it around himself and with an angry gesture strode out into the night.

Herodias stood at the door of her rude little house, tall and straight and silent, then turned back to the fireplace and sank down on the settle, shivering. This was a dreadful thing, like some frightful nightmare! She remembered the same feeling at Weymouth when, one winter's night, Hicks had gone out in a rage before, because she hadn't known how to skin the deer he had brought in, and had cut her hand and wept from fear and discouragement. She was only fifteen then. Now, of course, she was seventeen, and quite a woman grown.

As she sat there cowering under the dreadful fears of the dark future, the crying of a little child caught her ears. She forgot herself, and rushed to the door to see what could be the meaning.

"I've lost myself," cried the little boy—who must have been about five years old—"My father told me to walk ahead, and he would catch up to me! But he didn't come! Oh, I want to go home!"

Herodias took his little hand and finding he was the son of one of her neighbors, walked to his house, knocked, and when his mother opened the door, gave the little fellow over to her. In gratitude the mother asked her in. Mrs. Stanton was a kind woman who had just come to Newport. Her husband came in soon, greatly distressed at losing his little son. He was also grateful to Herodias and made her sit with them for a while. Their kindness touched Herodias deeply, and after the boy had been tucked in bed, she told the Stantons of her sad plight.

"You should have gone with your husband, said Mrs. Stanton.

"I do not think so. You do not know Hicks. He is glad to be free from petticoats. He told me at the Tavern that he was going on the first ship from Newport, and that he didn't want to be bothered with any girl on this trip, or ever again," said Stanton. "You must do the best you can, girl. We will see what can be done for you."

"John has my mother's money," said Herodias. "He told me it would be safer with him, and he would buy what I neded from what he would earn. Oh, why did I believe him! He seemed so kind in London! This cruel New England has made a cruel man out of him, and I have not been able to suit him. But I will not despair. I have God's spirit to guide me, as it has my people, and I will trust all the more to that!"

As she was leaving the house, a tall dark figure approached the door and Stanton's voice roared out:

"George Gardiner! By Gad, sir, but I am glad to see you! Take this young woman to her home, and then come in and warm your bones by our fire. Don't be too long, now. I'll be looking for you!"

Poor Herodias, feeling all out of place everywhere, thanked him in a low murmur and walked without more ado to her house just a street beyond. The tall man opened the door for her to enter and caught a glimpse of her sad, strained young face. He had never seen such a pair of eyes. Very eloquently they thanked him as she said "good-night and thank you, sir" and walked into her little house, closing the door behind her.

She had seen a face that haunted her. All through the dreadful night, the picture of Hicks, red with liquor and angry at her stubbornness, was constantly being followed by this tall, dark form towering over her as she closed the door of her little house!

Gardiner returned to Stanton's and inquired about the girl, and felt deep concern when told that Hicks had left her.

"She's too pretty to be left loose like that, Stanton; someone should take her in. Why don't you and your wife give her a home? She'll surely be gossiped about if she lives alone. Did you say she is a Quaker?" asked Gardiner.

"Yes, and not ashamed of it, by Gad!" It's a damned shame, one can't be widow or maid in this country. I'll tell you what we'll do, Gardiner; you need a wife; we'll ask her to stay here and if she suits you, why take her. What do you say? She's strong; I've seen her carrying pails of water and she can carry one on her head without spilling a drop, and she can spin, for my wife has seen her. Haven't you, wife?"

"Yes, she is fairly smart, but she didn't work hard enough for Hicks. She said her soul must be fed, too, you see, and she would go to Friends' Meeting," said Mrs. Stanton.

The next day, George Gardiner went away for a trip, to see some land he was interested in. It belonged to Indians and he hoped to interest Stanton, too. After a few weeks, he returned to Newport and found Herodias living still in her own little house. She had refused the Stanton's kind offer. Why should she not live alone if she wished! And manage her own home and not be a burden or worry to kind Mrs. Stanton!

She managed to knit stockings, and sell a few, to get food for herself. She was knitting away as nimbly as an old woman, when George Gardiner's loud knock startled her. It was late in the afternoon on a September day, and the sun was shining in the little window, very boldly, with its red, fiery face, making bright yellow patches on the wall.

Herodias brushed the stray hairs under her muslin cap and opened the door. There stood the tall, dark man, George Gardiner, over six feet, very broad of shoulder, face tanned, blue eyes laughing and pleasant mouth opening to say:

"Mistress Hicks, will you permit me to enter? I have somewhat to say."

Quite surprised, Herodias bowed and replied:

"It must be somewhat of importance, for as thou must know, I am poor and deserted by my husband and cannot buy aught and have nothing but stockings to trade for food and necessities. May I ask thee what is thy business?"

"Probably, Mistress Hicks, you have forgotten that I escorted you home from Mr. Stanton's one night some weeks ago. I am George Gardiner, come from England to help establish a land safe for white people, and have just returned from conferring with the Indians and looking over some lands which in some not far distant time will be lived in by our English."

"Why, Mr. Gardiner! Come in, sir, and tell me more about thy trip. Didst thou find any mountains of gold or silver?"

"No, nothing but granite, Mistress Hicks, granite and woods and streams."

"But, sir, how can this concern me?" asked Herodias.

"This is what I propose. I am a lonely man. You a lonely girl. I will give you a home and name again, if you could undertake to permit me. I must often be away, for I am a pioneer, as they call me, and they never stay home long! I have work to do to make a place for our people."

There was something magnetic about his enthusiasm. Herodias was greatly moved. Her knitting fell unheeded to the floor. George Gardiner stood up, and his head nearly touched the low ceiling. He took Herodias by the hand.

"Come now, Mistress Hicks, you are a Quaker! I know, for Stanton has told me. If I come here to see you and we be not man and wife, the neighbors will tattle and harm your character. It goes with knitting to tattle! So come with me to our good friends, the Stantons, and we will marry in your fashion, before witnesses, promising to take each other for husband and wife."

"Oh, I could not, Mr. Gardiner. You must know that I am still the wife of John Hicks. He might return and claim me."

"Never! If he has deserted you, it is not possible. If he went off and left you to starve or die and came back and found another man caring for you! It is not the custom here, in this wild country, to leave good women to shift for themselves, with so many fellows in need of a woman to keep their home for them. Come with me to the Stantons' and we will talk this over with them, if you like."

There are some women who were never intended to be alone and Herodias felt she must be one of them, as she put on her cape and quilted hood and meekly followed this domineering man to the door. He took her arm to hold her up over the icy stones and ruts of the street. For it was winter now, and the ground frozen with the foot-prints of the different creatures, horses or cattle, which had passed by during the recent rain and mud.

They found the Stantons seated before their fire. Mrs. Stanton was darning some mittens and Mr. Stanton cracking nuts. Both greeted their callers soberly, for something in their manner warned them of the seriousness of the visit.

"Stanton, I have decided to marry this young woman, and you and your wife must be the witnesses. What do you say?"

"Mr. Gardiner, I cannot be party to this," exclaimed Mrs. Stanton. "I am not a Quaker, and think you should have more of a record to show for future use, if need be. This is one reason the authorities in Massachusetts dislike the Quakers. What is there to show that you are really married, if you don't have it recorded.

"Oh, that will be all right," said Gardiner. "As I understand, the word of any Quaker is as good as his bond."

Mrs. Stanton insisted that she would not be responsible.

"Well, Gardiner," finally Stanton ended the discussion, "Stand up before me, both of you, and I'll do the best I can for you. Well do I know the cruel tongues of the gossips can torment and destroy the character of a saint, let alone a pretty, taking young woman, and it is the best solution of the problem of caring for Herodias that I know of."

So they stood before Robert Stanton, and promised before him to take each other for man and wife and live together as such. Mrs. Stanton continued to shake her head over it. She well knew that already Herodias had caused herself to be gossiped about for living alone. Of course, she could tell everyone she knew that Herodias had become the wife of George Gardiner, and hope for the best.

Very soon, the Gardiners went out, this time to the home of George Gardiner. It was the first time Herodias had been in such a house. It was much larger than her little home. The fireplace had a pair of silver candle sticks with real candles! Gardiner lighted them for Herodias. This was luxury to her.

The pine knots, which she had used, were not to be seen here. A bright, silver tankard was also on the mantle; several books were arranged on a shelf. Skins of deer, bear and wolf were thrown over the floor and a large, billowy feather bed showed in the corner, built like a berth on a ship! Riding boots and spurs were hung from a peg, and a closet shelf showed flour, cheese, spices and many jars of food stuffs. Beside the fireplace was a large jug of rum, and on one of the tall andirons rested a kettle of hot water, while on the other, there was a covered dish.

George drew the girl to his big chest, and gave her a warm embrace and hearty kiss; then, while her head rested on his strong arm, he looked long into her eyes and said;

"I'll do my best for you, Herodias. It's a hard world over here, and as I told you, I must be often away, but there is a chance here for a man and a woman! Sit down, and we'll see what there is in this dish for us! I took a chance you'd come home, if I needed you!"

So saying, he took the uncovered dish and two silver spoons, which he took from a secret cubby hole behind the fireplace, and they ate from the same dish their first meal together. It was meat and turnips cut small and well seasoned. Probably neither of them cared much what it was.

Newport, at that date, could furnish one with fish and mutton, corn and turnips and apples, grapes in season, and pork products; much salted food in the winter season. Molasses was to appear a little later and rum. Wines and beer were to be had also.

"Herodias, dear girl, I am happy to have you here! Travelling around as I do, it will be a comforting thought to picture a pretty, young wife waiting for me to come home. I may find your mountain of gold. I shall look hard for it. The Indians are very friendly around Narragansett, and proud to show anyone the beauties of their lands. How would you like to take a little trip over there with me some day?"

"Mr. Gardiner, I can't say how glad it would make me to tramp with thee through the beautiful country, when the spring comes. I must get my things from my little home, sir. Could we not get them tonight? — so that I might begin the new day with a new life with thee here?"

"Truly, we shall go now, but pray call me

George if I am to be your husband. I will get my horse and saddle bags to help bring your belongings."

"Perhaps, tomorrow, I may dare call such a stranger by his familiar name, but just now I can only think of thee as Mr. Gardiner, sir!"

"Just as you say for tonight" laughed Gardiner.

The girl amused him. He belonged to a noble family, with several older brothers, and no chance for inheriting his father's estate in England, and with an unsatisfied craving for exploring. He had been in many scrapes in England, but had come out of them whole skinned and cheerful with an optimistic vision and tremendous enthusiasm. Here, he hoped to establish a large estate and live like his older brother in England, after he had made money!

It was the dream of hundreds of these young Englishmen to become large land owners here in New England, and set up an English gentry. Herodias should be the mother of his children. To look at her, one would know she was of good stock to be a mother. The Longs in England were a good, old family, and but recently reduced in fortune. Herodias' voice and manners were fine and not coarse or of the common people—and her spirit was proved to be staunch in that she stood to face suffering rather than desert her faith and people.

That evening they moved the poor little possessions of hers to the new home, and it only took a few trips with the horse to bear the furniture. The table and chairs belonged in the house, as did the bed, so there were just the chest and spinning wheel and a few pots and pans, and her poor little collection of clothes, and it was all over. They were soon placed around, so that by curfew hour, the task of settling was done, and at eighteen, Herodias started her second chapter of life.

Pettaquamscutt

GARDINER, true to his word,—took her with him to see a high ridge of land in the Narragansett land. They took a strong row boat, and rowed to the long island called: "Conanicut," owned by Coddington and other gentlemen for sheep raising; then walked across due west to the further shore over the soft green meadows to a fisherman's cabin, and there borrowed his boat and rowed by the island, where the Dutch had their trading post, and Herodias was so afraid she might hear news of Hicks! The Dutch had used this island as a place to trade skins and shells from the Indians—just beyond to the west was "Namcook" or "Good Fishing" as the Narragansetts called it. They beached the boat there, and were soon surrounded by curious Indians.

Gardiner drew Herodias near his side protectingly, and with a smile, handed some bright glass beads and tin mirrors to the curious Indians, which they silently took and most seriously examined. When they understood that these trinkets were for them, they leaped with joy and behaved as happy, delighted children. The Indian maidens took Herodias by the hand, and she lost her fear of them.

Gardiner knew enough of their sign language to say that he and his wife wished to see the high lands to the west and the great rock of Pettaquamscutt. As soon as they learned this, they directed a lithe, active young Indian to guide them across the river. Through the fields they tramped, over the pastures where the horses and cattle were grazing, past the two ponds, and down the banks to the river. Here, their guide produced a canoe, hidden behind a sheltered cover, and paddled them across the river. Before them rose a high ridge of land extending for miles in either direction. On reaching the west shore, the Indian drew up the canoe and hid it in some bushes, and with long strides, proceeded them still westward but slightly south.

"I am tired, George," at last gasped Herodias! She was not used to such a hill. "I will give you a hand. How is that? — better, is it not?" As he spoke, Gardiner put his big hand at Herodias' back by the waist, and as if by magic, her fatigue was gone!

"How much that helps me, I could go on for miles,— why should that help so?" she asked.

"I don't know myself, but it is an old trick and doesn't seem to add a mite to my own endeavor. Here we are at last! Look about you and see this new country! Do you wonder I am always tramping around to see what more is to be seen!"

The Indian made a sign. Looking where he pointed, they saw several deer swimming down the river they had just crossed, pursued by a canoe filled with Indians, who were drawing bows with arrows, and as they looked, shot the largest stag behind the ear. There was a terrific panic in the water, fear giving the wild creatures wings to plunge about and dart into the thickets along the shore.

Gardiner examined the rocks on top of this high ridge, and exclaimed at the glittering streak in some. The Indian smiled, shaking his head, as if to say it was nothing.

"Do you know I think this may be gold, Herodias. Let us take some of this rock back to Newport and see if anyone can tell us about it." They passed through broad fields of corn, waving in the breeze on "Namcook" and groups of Indians seated, polishing shells for wampum in the shade of a few remaining pine trees. Some were making moccasins and making leather jackets from deer skin. They all looked gentle and peaceful, frequently smiling shyly at Herodias, as she walked back to the shores of Narragansett Bay, where George, being well pleased with his day's walk, was happy to pull the oars and quickly rowed her back to Conanicut. They drank deeply of the running brook on the hillside before getting into the boat. George had cheese and hard, dry bread in his deep pocket.

"I would be so happy if I could get land for a little farm over on that high ridge. Of course, it wouldn't be safe, would it, George, to live among the savages? They look peaceful enough, but I hear they are liable to go on the warpath once in a while and burn and torture most frightfully."

Gardiner replied, "You surely shall have a home on the side of that great hill—and we shall see the most beautiful view in the whole of this New England just as you have wished—although we may not find the gold. I do not fear the Indians if we are fair to them."

Newport News

THE Clarkes had brought warm clothing and bedding and necessities of living but of course at first there could be no luxuries.

Mr. Coddington had been married again soon after his first wife had died.

Mr. Dyer's wife was named Mary, a devoted supporter of Mrs. Hutchinson. She had left the church at the same time. She was deeply concerned over spiritual matters.

"Frances," Jeremy said to his wife one day, "it's not well to get too deeply agitated over these points of religion. I fear Mrs. Dyer and many others will come upon more trouble yet. It's a pity we cannot stay peacefully here and not tear our hearts and souls to pieces over things too obscure for us."

"It is true, my dear," replied Frances as she sat knitting before the huge glowing log, one foot regularly rocking the cradle in which the little Walter lay ready to drop to sleep for the night. "Mrs. Dyer reads and prays much; she discusses the questions which inquisitive persons ask her and argues till my head grows weary of it all and I long for the peace of our fireside."

"I was given a new task today. They have appointed me to assist Robert Jeffreys in taking up the accounts of the treasurer," said Jeremy.

"You should be good at that if you are at all like your uncle—Jeremy Weston. It would be pleasing to them, in old England, to have a colony which would repay them and not always send back sad acounts of themselves. There are surely a good number of peaceful folk here, at this end of the Island. Let us hope and pray for our success; I have great faith in you, Jeremy. Though not as old as some others, your calmness is like oil on troubled waters."

"Due to your good care and tenderness, dear wife. It's a sad life for the husbands of the stormy-tongued women."

This same year, he, with John Coggeshall and Robert Jeffreys, laid out the lots of land. Four acres were to be allowed each settler for his house and land for farming and grazing.

On Sabbath Day the colony met in the various dwellings, at first so rough, with not enough chairs to go round—Mr. Coddington, Mr. Easton, and Mr. Brenton in Newport, holding the Quaker Meeting.

In Portsmouth, Mrs. Hutchinson held meetings. Samuel Gorton, a man of strong personality but obscure views on religion began to attract some followers. He held sin to be spiritual and therefore separate from the physical, so that a man might kill a person by chance with no thought of hate or premeditation and be innocent of sin, while another might never actually kill, personally, but by hating in his soul in some unseen way bring about death and thus be guilty of the mortal sin of the soul, murder. Though much too advanced for the age, certainly the latter part of this theory was gospel teaching of Jesus.

The following year, in 1640, Mr. Samuel Gorton's maid-servant, having over-zealously guarded her master's pasture, when she beheld a strange cow grazing in his field, rushed angrily at the old woman who owned the cow. She is said to have beaten the old woman and torn out her hair. The Deputy Governor to whom the old woman complained, sent for Gorton's maid and bound her over to the Court.

"Mr. Gorton's mighty angry about it," Mr. Clarke told his wife, the evening after the trial. "You should have heard the excitement, Mr. Gorton felt that because his maid was of the servant class she was to be punished, not because she had disturbed the peace, or had behaved atrociously to the old dame. So, like many a man when he can say no more, he began to attack Governor Coddington whom he accused of being no friend of the King, saying, 'those who are for the King, throw out Mr. Coddington.' This was contempt of Court and the Governor spoke angrily back, 'Those who are for the King, remove this man.' So saying, Mr. Gorton was put out of the room and is to be sent from the Island. It's a shame for he only worked himself up to such a state in good part to protect the poor frightened servant-maid who was in a sad condition to be sure, over her quick temper. Mr. Gorton has in mind to go to see Mr. Williams and settle in some other place, not finding any group of religion exactly to his tastes here."

"I am sorry for Mrs. Gorton and the family, just settled in their new little home here," replied Frances. "He was so useful, too, knowing well how to cut cloth for the men's suits."

"It's true, many will miss him and he is the first to be driven out of Newport. It is not like the Governor to be so peppery. In attacking his loyalty to the Crown, Mr. Gorton touched upon a very sore spot, for it is well known, Coddington has many friends on both sides.

"Mr. Gorton will probably be whipped for his rude behavior and banished from Newport."

"It is well the colony is to have a school master; this ought to relieve the mothers, to know their children are being taught by a man used to the society of old England.

"They should like Mr. Lenthall, and I am happy he has been in the ministry for he will doubtless teach them good morals and good manners at the same time. It will keep them occupied through the winter months," said Frances.

"Anne Hutchinson is again being persecuted they tell me," continued Clarke, "I saw Captain Edward Gibbons with Mr. William Hibbens and John Oliver, today and they are sent here to inquire into certain affairs of our Island. Particularly to find the state of religion which they claim to be most irregularly carried on. Persons who have been excommunicated in Boston are holding meetings and partaking of the Communion among themselves. This, they say they have no right to do— poor Anne, never at peace with those irate ministers, even here. It's a pity they won't let us alone. They insist we men all carry arms, which you know is contrary to our belief. Why must they force their authority over us when we are beginning our life all fresh here?"

"There must be danger from the Indians, perhaps," suggested Frances.

"But they are friendly to us because we are fair to them and don't carry weapons. That has been our policy with them. Therefore they act their best selves when with us," said Clarke.

The following year a new little baby came to the Clarkes, a daughter named Mary, for her father's mother. Jeremy Clarke was elected freeman this same year, 1641, with William Freebone and others. Evidently the Massachusetts authorities exerted influence enough to persuade the Island that it must be prepared to defend itself, for the following spring, they elected Mr. Clarke Lieutenant of the Militia. Of course his sword and gun must be kept bright and clean and hung over the door. The Dungan children were delighted to see their step-father order his company in line and drill

on the Common. Mr. Coddington and Mr. Coggeshall and Lieutenant Clarke bought together a lot
of land, sixty-two acres, from Mr. Robert Carr.
This was on the East of Millbrook and bounded on
the south by the highway that goes to the Great
Common. So you may be sure that on the days of
the drill, the little Dungans would run down and,
themselves, line up to watch the patient drilling of
the Newport Company. It was a preparedness
parade at least, though lacking in perfect uniforms,
to be sure, their bright red coats and brass buttons
were mostly given in exchange for lands and in
trade to the Indians. The Quakers were wise in
wearing snuff-colored clothing and dark green—
very much safer for soldiers, too, especially in crossing fields and hiding behind trees and rocks. They
realized what a bright shining target their red and
brass made to an enemy. They were not inclined
to fight, but were required to be able to protect their
homes.

Mr. Hutchinson died this same year, 1642, and
his wife much chagrined and saddened resolved to
go to Long Island and live under Dutch protection.
The excitement and battle for her belief being
somewhat calmed at Portsmouth and the kind
influence of her very patient husband being now lost
to her, she must roam on further. So she started
forth with her children. She travelled to a place
near Hells Gate, Long Island where they were all,
except one daughter, within a year, murdered by

Indians shortly after Roger Williams' visit to Manhattoes.

Her sister, Mrs. Scott, in Providence, whose little daughter was to bear witness for her belief, Mrs. Mary Dyer of Newport, her most devoted disciple; Herodias Long Hicks who, with her husband, were firm followers, were all much grieved at her leaving the Island. In fact, John Hicks was so under her spell that he resolved to follow her to the Dutch. His wife refused to leave the protection of the English. She had been ill treated by Hicks who was a hard drinker and inclined to be ugly at such times, he had been sentenced to a fine for beating his wife and before that had been fined for drunkenness. On the Jury, at the time, was one, Mr. George Gardiner who was lately come to the Island. The young Quaker girl at this time impressed them all with her pitiful story and now no one blamed her for preferring the kindly atmosphere of Newport to wandering off with the rough and impulsive Hicks. Robert Stanton was a friend of George Gardiner's and together they undertook to look over the land across the bay. With John Porter they examined the shores and long ridge of rocks in the Narragansett Lands. Traces of coal were found in Portsmouth. What looked like gold was found at Petaquamscut. Great secrecy and hidden excitement was in the air. All sorts of possibilities were in this new country.

Of course Mr. Clarke heard these rumors, but

his conscientious character kept him closely confined with his increasing duties. For three years he was to be Treasurer of Newport; this came to him on January 18, 1644. Two months later, the good training of his company warranted his advancement from Lieutenant to Captain, the head of the Newport Militia. He was now thirty-nine, the father of a new little boy, Jeremy Clarke, Jr., making three of his own and four Dungan children—seven young to bring up and teach, feed and clothe.

Mr. Thomas Hazard was very busy overseeing the Indians who were filling in some land at the foot of the Spring, as they were to have ships' docks built along the water front. Here again the Indians preferred to be paid in brass buttons for their hard work. The Indians were very skillful at making stone-walls and toiling in the fields. The plantations from the first had to be cleared and walls built, seed planted, corn hilled. Mr. Easton's first rude little home had burned the second year after his arrival. He had secured a farm east of Newport on a high land, overlooking a magnificent beach with the ocean beyond and a view of Seaconnet in the eastern horizon. Mr. Coddington was the largest land-owner, having finally acquired about seven hundred and fifty acres from the Northwest to the Cove, Northeast as far as Miantinomis Hill. Here he had many sheep, both black and white, a number of cattle and horses. Much of his land was covered with spruce, pine, and hemlock, with some maple and oak trees. He counted on getting eighty bushels of corn to an acre. He had a large house in town with a hall through the centre and an over-hanging second story. Next to this large property was Mr. Brenton's farmland of about four hundred acres. After a few years he changed his farm to the land south and east of the town. Mr. Clarke had much to do on his plantation, which, though not as large, furnished him with wheat, rye, barley and beans. Some hemp and flax also grew on the Island. Then there were apples, hickory and chestnuts, honey, wild strawberries and blackberries. The house-wives made their own butter and cheese. Pork, fowl and plenty of fresh fish made a generous diet. It must have been very hard on the cows and horses, who had to be the pioneer breeders and cross the Atlantic. On some rough trips nearly all the animals died before they arrived on these shores.

Barbara Dungan, Frances' oldest child, married James Barker, destined to be Ensign in 1648-9— Governor's Assistant, nine years—Deputy Governor of Newport for fourteen years.

Frances, these years, was attending strictly to the enormous task of bringing forth new little Clarkes. In 1645 young Latham Clarke was born,—four little Clarkes and three of them boy babies,—what a proud father and what a busy mother! Of course Mr. Clarke was prominent in the affairs of the Colony. At this time, Mr. Coddington was having a law suit with Mr. Jeremy Gould, over quite a large sum of money at that time in Newport. Among the eight men chosen to deliberate over this case were Roger Williams and Jeremy Clarke. In October 1646, Mr. Gould acknowledged that he was debtor to Mr. Coddington for the sum of £1,000.

In 1647 a very exciting ballot was cast electing Mr. John Coggeshall as President of the Colony, assisted by Roger Williams, representing the Plantation of Providence, John Sanford of Portsmouth, William Coddington of Newport, Randall Holden of Warwick, William Dyer as General Recorder, and Jeremy Clarke as Treasurer. They undertook to draw up a suitable code of laws. This soon changed the next year and William Coddington was chosen President with Jeremy Clarke as his assistant. Roger Williams at this time was living in Wickford where he had a trading-post.

The voyage of Roger Williams to England produced his book, "The Key to the Indian Language," which he gave to Gregory Dexter, master-printer in London, to print for him. Probably in Mr. Dexter's printing shop Mr. Williams met the Poet Milton who was, like himself, a "Seeker." Sir Harry Vane was in Parliament, actively advocating toleration in Religion. The handsome young man had certainly been beloved by Mrs. Hutchinson and Mrs. Mary Dyer for his gentle, kindly courtesy and respect for the Quaker ideas. While Governor of Massachusetts he had aided the men and women with his counsel, moved by the zeal of their opinions regarding different points of religion. He saw their distractions, pitied their perplexities and worked for their interests and was himself a martyr at last.

"Things are getting very unsettled all over the country," said Mr. Clarke to his wife one day as they sat at the long board partaking of their noon-day dinner. "The government in England is in a dreadful state of rebellion, churches are being used for stables, the soldiers of Cromwell have smashed beautiful images and destroyed priceless paintings, calling them works of Satan. This is going too strong. Governor Coddington offended many. when he obtained the charter for the Island to keep it in its present state for his lifetime at least and had himself made Governor for life. There are many here who like him not, the Baptists especially. He has so enraged them that even our good friend Dr. John Clarke has joined with Roger Williams in protesting the Charter. They have made me Governor in his place with title of "President Regent." This is done to disturb the government as little as possible since I had been the Governor's Assistant. Of course he has been my friend and I stand by him in this because I understand what he means by it. He wants to keep this settlement calm and safe although all the colonies in New England should change for Cromwell to-morrow and for the King the following day."

"Oh, I am so troubled over this," sighed Frances. "Here we are with these young children and the whole world across the seas in England turned upside down. I can't bear to think of the Judges actually putting King Charles to death. If you had known him as a young fellow riding over the moors with my father, carrying his falcon, you would feel sorrowful indeed."

A baby boy was born the following month in April. The last son had been named for her family, so this new little brother was named for Mr. Clarke's mother's family, Weston.

Through these perilous days the Island's affairs continued to prosper, the population increased, but the disturbances over-seas were felt by many in different ways on this side of the Atlantic. With party feeling rising—Royalists and Parliamentists, Sectarianists also took more offensive sides. Special wrath was beginning to descend upon the Quakers, who braced with all their spiritual powers against it, proudly, joyously braving punishment and persecution. So far Newport had been attacked through Mrs. Hutchinson and now through Mr. Coddington as the impersonation of Quakerism. It is no wonder that this next year when still another little son, James Clarke entered the world, that he should be destined to be a minister. This little baby was followed two years later by a second daughter Sarah, born in 1651, and this child completed the number of two daughters and five sons for the most worthy and estimable Jeremy Clarke.

Quakers at Newport — 1651

THERE must be something pacific in the balmy air of Newport. Here we find the Baptists far less unkind to their Quaker neighbors. Mr. John Clarke, Baptist preacher and physician, wrote about this time:—

"Notwithstanding the different understandings and consciences amongst us, without interruption we agree to maintain civil justice and judgment; neither are there such outrages committed amongst us as in other parts of the country are frequently seen."

Dr. Clarke had always been a friend of Mr. Coddington and Mr. Dyer and Mr. Coggeshall from 1640 when they formed themselves into a church fellowship with Dr. Clarke officiating. Owing to the different beliefs, the following year, it had seemed best to separate into two churches, Mr. Lenthall, the school teacher, holding rather upsetting ideas and leaving Newport as a result. Coddington, Easton, Brenton and others gave their houses for the Friends' meetings as the record of the Quaker meetings tell us. Dr. Clarke led the first Baptist group. Being a true Pacifist and doing his best to keep peace in the State of Rhode Island and the Plantations and finding the political and religious parties becoming too turbulent, Dr. Clarke agreed with Mr. Roger Williams to go to England and procure a charter which would bring peace to all. Mr. Williams was politically and religiously antagonistic to Mr. Coddington and was bitterly condemning of the Quakers. So it is coincidental that his voyage to England to wrest the Government of Rhode Island from such an opponent—a Quaker—should happen to be the year Rhode Island felt her worst attacks against her Quakers.

Governor Endicott in Massachusetts was this year, 1652, actively engaged in extending his state boundaries. With Roger Williams in England this same year primarily to have Coddington's charter repealed, also on some private business of his own, we find Mr. Coddington getting into more criticism on account of his dealings with the Dutch. Letters from Peter Stuyvesant, Dutch Governor of Long Island and Ensign George Baxter, containing an offer to furnish soldiers to be used on Rhode Island, was held as a charge of conspiracy. The bearers of the letters were held in bail for £100 till they were proved innocent. It is not improbable that the cordial relations between the Dutch and Quakers led to this offer. Captain Andrew Willett was well known to them and used to settle boundary disputes around Oyster Bay, for both the English and the Dutch. The English Revolution threatened all the settlements and although Mr. Coddington was attacked many times by his political and religious enemies, he was again and again placed in high position over his enemies and died a Governor.

President Clarke and Walter

JEREMY CLARKE was certainly feeling the heavy responsibility of life. No wonder, he loved to take his little son Walter, now thirteen years old, and, leaving these scenes, stroll along the rocky cliffs called Purgatory and let the wind blow over his troubled brow.

Walter was at the age when he aspired above all things to be a man like his father. He watched every move and gesture and in his own mind compared him with some kings of England, especially Alfred whom he had read many tales about. On one special afternoon when his father returned from the town, looking particularly careworn, the boy said to him, "Let's go for a ride, father." The idea pleased Mr. Clarke. At once his brow cleared of its troubled look, he brushed back his light brown hair, slightly gray around the temples, and with a boyish smile reflected for a moment his eager young son's fresh face.

Frances loved him like this. She asked before they left for the ride, "What has happened, Jeremy?" To which he replied,

"You know Dr. Clarke and Mr. John Crandall and Mr. Obediah Holmes went over to Swampscott to cheer Mr. William Witter, the blind old Quaker. Over a month ago Mr. Witter had been severely reprimanded for speaking his views against Infant

Baptism. Mr. Clarke preached a sermon in Mr. Winter's house, on the subject of Patience under Temptation. Someone from here must have told of the intended visit for, in the midst of the preaching, two constables arrived with a warrant signed by the magistrate, Robert Bridges, and arresting our friends, carried them to the Governor. There they ordered them to go to the Meeting House. Not wishing to cause trouble they entered while the people were praying. They removed their hats as long as the praying lasted.

"Putting them on, when the prayer was finished, they sat down and Dr. Clarke proceeded to read his Bible. Now see what Dr. Clarke did. At the end of the service he arose and turning to the congregation, told them that he 'could not judge that they were walking or meeting according to the order of the Lord.' This produced a highly indignant commotion and the three men were marched back to the Ale House. They told me they were guarded 'like thieves and robbers' for a month, then taken to court where John Endicott tried them. Rev. John Cotton tried to exhort them. They received a sentence of a fine or severe whipping. Can you believe it!'"

By this time some of the little Clarkes were sobbing; they loved and admired Dr. Clarke, and Mr. Holmes was a frequent visitor at their home. The thought of their suffering a *whipping* was too much for their tender hearts. They knew nothing of the dreadful teaching that Hell was paved with the skulls of unbaptized infants! They had never seen the frightful pictures depicting the devils with red skins and horns and forked tails dragging persons to a yawning fiery pit. Such pictures had been shown to illustrate God's punishments to the wicked. Here on Rhode Island the teaching of religion was kindness. The mental torments inflicted on tender souls by the cursed teaching of bigoted ministers over-zealous in their efforts to save souls may require a sad explanation at the Great Day of Judgment. It is for God Himself to judge if a man, woman or little child be bad! And the Quakers believed this to be a very serious sin, for it was more or less damning. For a little child to be told he belonged to the Devil or was Bad took away his Hope— Dante put this sentence over the door of Hell, "All Hope abandon ye who enter here!" The motto of Rhode Island is "Hope."

Milton himself wrote feelingly from his observations, "The Devil can quote scripture to his purpose."

"Go on, father, tell us all."

"Dr. Clarke seriously asked to see the law by which they could be whipped. This request 'somewhat transported' Mr. Endicott who called Dr. Clarke 'Trash' and 'deserving death': rather strong words! Friends offered to pay the fine of Dr. Clarke and Mr. Crandall who were released on bail, but listen well: Obediah Holmes was actually whipped with thirty lashes. He said 'I bless God I am counted worthy to suffer for the name of Jesus.' Imagine, the Pastor of the Boston church struck him and cursed him saying, 'The curse of God go with thee.' He told me, he had slept well the night before, had refused to drink wine. Mr. Endicott after a delay, failing to arrive, the man who was to apply the lash was told to proceed by Mr. Increase Nowell.

Obediah Holmes walked forward with his testament in his hand. He was stripped to his waist, then his hands bound to the whipping post. The executioner spat three times on his hands and applied the lash made of three cords plied three times. Thirty blows! When it was over, Mr. Holmes turned to Mr. Nowell with a face bright with religious joy and said to him 'you have struck me as with roses.'

"The people around were greatly aroused by his patient and dignified bearing and much sympathy was expressed for him. His back was so badly cut by the cruel lashes, that for many days and nights he was unable to rest save on his hands and knees, the lash cutting around his waist. A number of his friends accompanied him back here and my heart and soul are grieved indeed to think of the bitter hatred which is in the hearts of many against the Quakers."

"Come, father, let's ride," insisted young Walter, holding the door open for his father.

With a sigh the man on whose shoulders the Government of the Island was resting, turned toward the sunshine and looking down into the eager eyes of his boy caught the faith and fearlessness and unconquerable spirit of his youth. "Ah, well, my son, we must get our exercise and have a view of the Ocean. Come, Walter, and we shall pretend we are King Alfred and his father going across Europe while we sit a while on the distant rocks and watch the waves dash themselves to pieces."

Away they clattered through the little streets of Newport with the rough cobble stones, by the common, on by Mr. Arnold's old stone mill, across to the cliffs and out along the high plains to the rocky end of the Island. Dismounting, they let their horses browse. Mr. Clarke sat down silently for a moment, looking far off in the direction of his old home England. The boy sat nearby throwing a few stones into the restless ocean which, ever receding and gathering itself up to throw itself in futile effort against the rocks, only succeeded in dashing itself to myriads of tiny particles of spray which fell back upon itself unceasingly.

"That shows how turmoils, wars, ravings and all the wild, ungoverned elements of man can not alter the rock of Everlasting Truth—only tear mankind to pieces and throw it back upon itself to be calm and patient—remember, that, Walter. Be calm and patient."

"Tell me a little about King Alfred, father, we are to have him in our history tomorrow. I know he is one of your favorite heroes."

"He is so because he had many of the same problems we have to face, my son: a new chance, the great responsibility of setting up wise laws for a framework for the new enterprise. I would like to take you across the great ocean to see how our civilization compares with the Old World systems. Alas . . . All seems so upset in England yet . . ."

"But, father, tell me more about Alfred and his father's travels . . . What happened?'"

"A very strange unexpected thing happened . . . We are apt to think of Alfred as a detached young man living in England. Let me tell you how Continental he really was. When Charlemagne was crowned, in 800, Emperor of Western Europe, Alfred's grandfather Aetheline, that same year, was crowned King of the West Saxons. He had lived for thirteen years as a youth in Charlemagne's service. His son, Aethelwolf, was greatly influenced by the Church and was crowned King of the Kents twenty-eight years later. Now King Aethelwolf had a cup-bearer named Oslac. A most trusted man was a king's cup-bearer. In those days Christianity was a tender plant growing fair and pure among rank and poisonous weeds. The Barbarians became suddenly converted but their wicked customs had not yet ceased to endanger the cultivation of the Christian virtues. Even among Christian rulers, it was general to remove the competitors for the Throne . . . Sometimes they were given distant lands to rule over. Sometimes they were poisoned. . . So a king's cup-bearer had to taste first before offering his King the cup. . . If he fell dead, well, that showed the King that his life had been attempted. . .

"Aelthelwolf was very fond of Oslac and had him constantly with him. The beautiful daughter of Oslac found great favor in the King's eyes and he thought of her so lovingly that he married her. Her name was Osberga. Alfred was born several years after, 849. When he was six years old, he went on this voyage to Rome to visit the Pope, Louis IV, who was his God-father. Ealston was Bishop of Sherbourne and Swithern, Bishop of Winchester. Both were very influential over the King of the Saxons.

"On the way to Rome, as befitted their rank and station, they visited the Court of Charles the Bald, Charlemagne's grandson. Here was a fascinating maid named Judith, thirteen years old, daughter of King Charles, tall, vivacious, captivating. . . What happened is hard to believe, but true, nevertheless. Alfred's father, then nearly sixty, was captivated by the maid and the following year in October they were married. The elderly bridegroom though brave and handsome had lived through hard battles with Danish Pirates and his age began to show deep and serious signs. After two years of companionship with his young wife, Judith—who was sixteen by this time—he died. · The young widow scandalized the family by marrying Alfred's brother, Aethelbald, later in the same year. This marriage ended sadly enough in the death of Aethelbald, three years later, when Judith returned to France, later eloping with Baldwin the Iron Arm—a Flemish noble. All this produced a rather turbulent home life for young Alfred, by this time only eleven years old. The influence of Church was strong in his life. As he grew older he tried to live a truly Christian life."

"How especially, father?" asked Walter.

"He had married Ethelsintha who was a faithful devoted wife and mother. All of their several children grew strong and lived fine lives. I hope my children do the same, my son. If you knew how much good it does to a father's heart to know his son is honest, brave and kind, and how a father detests and despises lies, cowardice and cruelty. That is why we punish these faults so severely."

"I want to know more about King Alfred. What was he like, do you know?" asked Walter eagerly looking into his father's face.

"He was tall and fair with large blue eyes. His friends were Churchmen. He made a vow to give half his time to God's service 'which vow with all his might he performed by day and night.' He had candles and lanterns made to measure the hours. Six candles lasted for 24 hours. As a young fellow he was especially fond of the Psalms of David and he kept his body under strict discipline as a Temple of God. And, happily for the country, there was

peace between Church and State. His fighting was
mostly with the Danes. Finally Guthrom, the Vik-
ing, sued for peace. Alfred had the pleasure of
standing as Godfather and naming him Aethelstan.
He also gave the Danes the Eastern part of Anglia
to live in. This is all very like our life, here, my
son. You know how we are trying to convert the
Indians on the Island without fighting, by showing
them our own lives lived in Peace."

"Yes, I know, father, and it must be hard for
you to see how cruelly the Massachusetts Christians
treat our Quakers. It will have a bad effect on the
Indians, won't it?"

"Indeed it will, even now they are finding the
Christians fight and hate each other and all our
teaching is vanishing before their councils. They
sit around their fires and smoke in silence, listening
and thinking, as one after another of their warriors
recounts the dreadful doings of the English among
their own people."

After a short time as the fog began to blow over
the Island, Mr. Clarke and Walter cantered back
through the town and putting up their good horses
entered their home. Walter, alive with grand ideas
for the future, glowing with ruddy rush of clean
young blood, burst open the door, which entered
into the great room of the house.

Mr. Clarke sadly and wearily followed his boy.
He had not felt well. His head was troubled over
the perplexities and divisions. He couldn't understand what had come over the whole Island. The

enemies of Mr. Coddington were working for his overthrow. Mr. Gorton had appeared again at Portsmouth. Benedict Arnold had newly come to Newport. Many new complexities threatened to change the Peace of the Island.

Like many a strong man who is left to support a bridge which is in danger of toppling, Mr. Clarke fell ill and died this same year in November,—just before his forty-sixth birthday,—one of Newport's finest and foremost founders.

His death is recorded in the Friends' meeting book of records in the Newport Historical Society:

"Jeremiah Clarke, one of the first Planters of Rhode Island died at Newport in said Island and was buried in the tomb that stands by the street on the water side of Newport, on the day of 11th March 1651."

The funeral was a very sad procession. Such a large number of children—of course, little Sarah was not a year old and remained in her cradle—with little Weston only three and a half, holding Frances' hand, Latham, six, Jeremiah, Jr., eight, walking hand in hand; Mary ten and Walter thirteen, followed by Barbara Dungan and her husband James Barker, William, Frances and Thomas Dungan, with their loyal friends. They walked the short distance to the Friends' Burying Ground on Farewell Street. What a heavy task for Mrs. Frances Clarke, the second time a widow, with a baby still in the cradle. Walter from this day became his mother's right-hand man.

One Hundred

Gorton's Influence

NEWPORT had a small revolution of her own the next year. The followers of Gorton were working for him in every way. Warwick and Providence elected Mr. Gorton, President, soon after Roger Williams left to get Coddington's charter repealed. They accused Mr. Easton of having deserted his office as President of Providence Plantations, accused Newport and Portsmouth of falling off from the established order of civil government by means of the commission presented to Mr. Coddington.

The Duke of York afterwards James II was granted all the lands of Alexander and much more which he sold and granted, even in Rhode Island. This explains Mr. Coddington's desire for a charter. He did not obtain the Island of Rhode Island but did obtain governorship for life, hoping to keep the Island for the People.

John Paine was granted Prudence Island, Mr. Gorton and his associates Warwick.

Sir Edmund Andros was set over the whole of New England and heartily disliked.

Captain Richard Morris led the rebellion in Newport. While the Governor sat in court, in Mr. Coddington's house, as there was no court house at that time, the men entered with force and told them to disperse. Mr. Coddington had always been friendly with the Dutch and because the Duke of York, Mr. Gorton's patron, had now become king and had ordered the English to drive out the Dutch from Manhattan and all New England, anyone friendly with them was viewed with suspicion. The Government in England was almost certain to be under the power of Cromwell's parliament. Coddington hoped to hold the Island from all its enemies. It gave great promise, as a commercial port, for unlike Boston, its harbour was never entirely frozen in the coldest of winter weather. Winthrop on one side, Connecticut on the West, Gorton and Williams on the North, all tried at the same time to wrest the control from Rhode Island.

It is no wonder that the poor little children of Frances Clarke were told to come in directly their bell was sounded, that Mrs. Clarke kept them with her as much as possible. They heard much of all this disturbance being serious minded as were most all the children of the day. A rule of anarchy was on the Island. Captain Patridge, a close friend of Mr. Coddington, had taken possession of a house, when twenty rough men and youths entered carrying guns, swords and staffs and drove him out, after which he was taken prisoner by Indians and hanged. Mr. Coddington appealed to Mr. Winthrop for aid and at last left the Island for the protection of Massachusetts where Gorton and his men did not follow him. This reign of terror in Newport continued for some time. Mr. Coddington's charter commission had not been recalled even though such an important person as Roger Williams was using every power he possessed. The fact that the Island had repudiated Mr. Coddington so that he was now living in Boston, added to the general lack of unity, more pronounced than ever among the Plantations of Portsmouth, Warwick, Pawtuxet, Narragansett and Providence. All these facts made for trouble enough for our heroine.

Frances and Her Children

ELEVEN lovely children were her care and comfort. There was not much time left for vanities after the day was over for the mother. When the children were tucked in their feather beds and trundle beds and some rolled up near the glowing fire, they unanimously slept. But little idea of the anxiety of such a mother can be given by the greatest stretch of our imagination, we who have but to telephone for instant help from druggist and physician. At first John Clarke was the only doctor we know of in Newport. John Cranston, a young fellow sent from London to be under Capt. Jeremy Clarke's care, had become much interested in the care of the sick and injured. He had an opportunity to see the good Dr. John Clarke work over the people in Newport. This determined him to become a Doctor himself later after he married Frances' little daughter Mary! If it was croup or measles or heavy cold—whatever it might be—the mother was the natural nurse. The fine out-of-door life of Frances as the Falconer's daughter gave a strong constitution to all of her children, eleven of whom grew up and married and furnished sons and daughters for our State.

When she sat lonely after an especially tiring day, she thought of the days when her husband had come home from his meetings with the Governor and important men of the Colony and had told her of his new responsibilities. How terrified she had felt when he was made Lieutenant and later Captain of the company at Newport. How possibly he would be a target for some Indian, though it was remarkable that, with so many around, they gradually withdrew from the Island, leaving very little to fear in that direction. Still, watch must be kept and drill regularly held in order to keep up the respect of the Red Men. Their chiefs were their great men and must deal with white chiefs as their equal. So Jeremiah's mailed vest and gun must be kept clean and oiled for instant use. She recalled when she first arrived on Rhode Island she was never without anxiety when on the dark winter afternoons with the terrors of the wilderness came the howl of wolves. Now and then the Indians would creep around for food or warmth. Those long winter evenings with the glowing log meant a close tie for the families and it was the mother who must give the touch to the conversation and the turn of thought, many times averting disputes within the home. For even then when children were repressed from their birth and quite grown up by twelve and taught to be seen but not heard, taught to be godly and to loath and to despise wickedness including all the vanities—they had a strong example in hearing their elders discuss the various sides of the finest points of religion. So that when they imitated their parents, as all little children do, and got a little excited over their opinions, it was much as it is today.

We may well imagine what comfort it was to tell of the scenes of her childhood, as Frances and her children tramped over the fields and saw the hawks far off. There is one special place near Third Beach beyond Paradise Rock where there always are to be seen the rough nests of the hawks. What more natural than that Frances should show her young son, Walter, how to tame one and use it for getting quail which were so plentiful in the brush thereabout. On hot summer days they all had a picnic and bath on the clean, sandy beach and surely there were clam bakes, for that was something the Indians could teach them to like, and corn roasts. Those must have been the great holidays. But their life was filled mostly with stern tasks for every one, from four or five in the morning till nightfall—no breakfasts served in bed for Frances or the mothers who laid the foundations of Rhode Island homes.

Walter had absorbed his father's spirit. This was shown in his after life. Every first son adores his father as a result of the pride and love given him from his birth. Never a man who was not completely elated at the birth of a healthy boy of his own, and never a little boy who did not with all his heart try to be a big man like his father, when he was truly only a little fellow. If his father smokes, he must need smoke; if he struts and swears, the little fellow must try to do so. This is more often lost when the boy grows up if his father lives, than if his father is taken from him at an early age, as was the case with Walter. They get to know each other better and often the very traits most like the father might come between the two. Frances was very happy in watching her sons develop into young men.

Many a warm summer afternoon was spent along the rocky shore of Newport. Here Frances could sit with her hands busily knitting while the children could climb over the rocks left wet with salt and covered over with prickly barnacles. Sometimes one of the children would fall down to come weeping to her. She would bind the poor little knee with her handkerchief after drying the tears. Then after they had gathered enough snails and perhaps a star fish or horse-shoe crab and lots of dulce and ribbon seaweed to play horse with and were glad to sit down, Frances would tell them of great people who had lived across the ocean.

Walter was always acquiring knowledge. He asked, "How do people get rid of their enemies now, mother?"

"My son, there are many ways. The simplest in this New World, seems to be by banishment, driving them from the settlements for Indians and wild animals to destroy. But see how God changes their cruelty. For this colony here, my son, is made up of persons who were considered enemies of Massachusetts, but here we live in a state where love and peace are the ideals. Your father said we were growing strong and increasing every way. I am hoping that you all will grow to be the finest kind of men and women, dear children, so that you may leave a name above reproach for all time associated with this New World."

"I mean to be a great man some day like my father, a great help to my mother."

"I wish you would tell us about Matilda. You started to the last time we came here, mother, when the storm came up so suddenly we had to run for shelter to the Easton's, don't you remember?" this from Mary.

"Matilda was taught to sew just as you are, my dear daughter. Many times I tell you to 'Love your Duty, and Do your Duty.' Be happy doing it. So Matilda wisely directed the work for her maids and gave them a great task.

"Matilda was industrious as you must be, darling daughter. See how much your mother has knit since you have been playing about. While her husband, William of Normandy, was spending his time fighting, with the idea of conquering England, this industrious wife gathered about her the ladies of her court who were very sad and lonely at being left without their dear husbands. Matilda suggested that they should work in tapestry the story of these wars which should be a picture for future reference."

"How long is the tapestry, mother? Could I make it, do you suppose?"

"Not in your lifetime, child. It is two hundred and thirty feet long, and twenty inches high. There are one thousand five hundred figures in it. Matilda presented it to Odo, the Bishop of Bayeaux, for his Cathedral. Odo was a half brother of William the Conqueror. That is a remarkable thing dear, for of course William would give his possible enemies positions of high power to keep their eyes off his throne. So Odo was kept very busy with the affairs of the Church. Lots of lace bonnets are made at Bayeaux, where the Cathedral is located."

"That is very interesting, mother; now let us play Indians"; and off they would rush for their favorite game.

There were many thoughts in her mind, as Frances sat there gazing out across the limitless space of dancing waves. Sometimes all dazzling silver and sometimes like an army of angry, raging, frothing horses, drawing chariots of Neptune's armies, dashing the elements of water into finest vapor. It rested her own turbulent thoughts when life seemed very, very hard and the trials of her faith were strong. After a night of mental conflicts, it was soothing to her to watch the heavy water turned into this soft mist, transformed into something which could be lifted up and floated high in the heavens, later to be rolled into clouds which would give showers to help the harvests. So her own selfish problems through terrifically hard battlings might be lifted up, with God's grace, and after being rested in the heavens, return in some good way upon her loved ones.

The sea—what an enchantment! How ever and always it beckons to the adventurous ones to trust themselves to its call. How like a great mother it was at times—carrying the ships on her deep-breathing bosom,—how like a woman lost in deep anger and passion, blind to consequences of harm and destruction done to those trusting in her benevolence. How gentle, when, her temper spent, she lies exhausted, reflecting the loveliest smiles and most enchanting colors, which kind heaven, her lord and master, shows on his face—thoughts too great for utterance. Only those who love to gaze upon her wide horizon can experience the grand inspiration and mental expansion felt rather than expressed.

Restless or calm, always in its depths containing unknown secrets!

Then back to her task of bringing up those treasures entrusted to her for guidance, with her thoughts swept clear of all the care of the petty, wearing little trials that crush down a woman's soul. It was just as necessary for Frances to get out to the vastness of the blue sky and dancing sunlight as to have food and clothing.

After the death of her husband especially, her own life became more lonely and her happiness and peace of mind was found only in daily care for her household.

One Hundred Eleven

JOHN CRANSTON
COAT-OF-ARMS

John Cranston Chooses His Wife

MARY CLARKE, now a lovely young girl of seventeen, helped Frances in the many duties of bringing up her younger brothers and little sister Sarah. Such a number of stockings to knit, so many household duties in the home; but as she walked demurely through the town be sure her bright eyes did not fail to notice every one. In fact, the Quakers were so observing that it was thought best to have a special bonnet made for the girls and women. It fitted close to the back of the head and protruded a long way around their face forward, so that it was almost impossible to see who was inside. This was supposed especially to help in keeping the minds of the young and old men from wandering in their Sabbath Meetings and, also, to keep the eyes of the maids and women from straying over to the opposite side of the room and interfere in any way with holy thoughts!

In spite of this precaution Cupid, the sly fellow, managed to ply his trade.

A certain Scotchman in Newport was destined to choose this seventeen year old Mary Clarke for his wife. John Cranston from London, son of James Cranston, Chaplain to the unfortunate King Charles I.

Walter Clarke was much interested in talking with John Cranston.

"Tell me John, why the Settlement of the Scotch is faring so badly?"

"Well, Walter, it's a long story but ye know in order to colonize a new territory someone must pay and certainly the Scotch have been sacrificed. Bonnie Queen Mary, because of her love for the French, had her beautiful neck cut from her shoulders and now the cruel English must kill my King Charles in like bloody manner. Cromwell must lead his men into the churches smashing the holy vessels and statues. Even so the Baronetcys sold by Alexander to so many brave and hardy Scotchmen are being discounted and the Barons themselves have been persecuted. The French extend their boundaries so that Nova Scotia is no longer a place for a Scotchman. You must know that our kinsman William Cranston was knighted by King James VI of Scotland for his bravery and success in driving off the lawless fellows from the Borders of Old Scotland. With twenty-five men he succeeded in holding order and punishing the lawless. The Scotchmen in Nova Scotia were to defend the Border against the French. But if Charles II marries the sister of the King of France it means no dowry for him if the Borderland of New France is troubled by Scots."

"You do well to speak of the importance of Boundaries," replied Walter Clarke, "with the men of Narragansett petitioning Connecticut to take them under their protection and the Massachusetts people looking longingly at our fertile island with its increasing sheep and cattle. I myself think Mr. Coddington very wise to go to Cromwell's Parliament and try to secure Governorship for his lifetime. If Charles does succeed in returning from France and sells the plantations over our heads we may find ourselves in a pretty state of affairs."

"It hardly seems possible you are going to marry Mary, such a young woman! But she has loved you when as a little bit of a girl, she would watch you beating the drum on the Common in the drills when my father was Captain."

"Well I remember," said John Cranston. "My father you know was a clergyman of the Episcopal Church. He had the benefice of St. Mary's Overy in Southwark, London. It was near the Bridge. When the Revolutionists drove my father out he had a very hard time of it getting food even for us, so sent me here to Newport to be under the care of your father."

"Aye, he was a Merchant when a Citizen of London. I hear you want to be a physician, John."

"In truth, I am studying the books which tell me all I can hope to learn and in time I may be a physician."

All this time the women were lighting the little candles. It took a half hour to light the first one, then the little Betty lamp, filled with tallow oil, hanging from the fireplace. Mary, with her full homespun skirt pinned back and her large apron on, leaned over the huge kettle to light the fire in the brick oven. The evening was growing chilly and the glow from the fire was very welcome. It threw dancing lights on her happy young face, flushed with the effort of putting in the wood and blowing the tiny spark to a blaze! When well heated, that is, after burning all night, the oven would be hot enough. She could put in the food for Sabbath Day. The quick baking pies first and the pot of beans last. They would bake slowly all Saturday night and be delicious with a piece of pork to moisten them. Mrs. Clarke was looking over her worsteds. The bright yellow dyed with onion skins, the duller yellow with goldenrod, the russet dyed with sumack, the brown dyed in the copper kettle! These were to be woven into new dresses for Mary's wedding chest! It was very charming to watch the spinning of the wool. Such a thoughtful occupation. It must be handled so carefully. Mary had found it very hard to keep her thoughts from day dreaming. She seemed to see John Cranston when she should be seeing the wool thread!

Mary married John Cranston in 1658 seven years after her father's death. Young Jeremy was fifteen, Latham was thirteen, Weston was ten, James nine, little Sarah seven. So Frances still had quite a task.

We may as well say here that John was a good student and after their marriage he did get a license to administer physic and practice chirurgery throughout the whole colony and was recorded "Doctor of Physic and Chirurgery."

Newport News

JOHN RICHMOND had come to Newport from Taunton. There had been a growing demand for timber to be sent to the settlements by water. Mr. Richard Smith in Wickford had built his house from logs floated down from the Taunton woods. John Alden in Plymouth was turning out very fine chairs, being a skilled carpenter. Because these colonists had intelligence they could adapt themselves to the needs of their little communities.

"Mother, where is Dr. Clarke?" asked Walter when they were together. "He has not been here since father's funeral. I know he went to England but isn't he ever coming back?'"

"There are many changes since then, my son. He was sent to England to see about a permanent Charter, because the people were so aroused over the Coddington Charter. We should have been a much more orderly State under Mr. Coddington. It has been dreadful and so upsetting. Sir Henry Vane has sent a pathetic letter urging all to live in peace, as the noise of the brawls in Providence and our town has reached far away England. Perhaps Dr. Clarke will never get a charter to his liking. With the Revolution in England, everything is unsettled. It grieves me to think they could kill their king. You know that my own father was his sergeant Falconer, that Mr. Cranston's father was his Chaplain. They might have dethroned him if he had been wicked, but to kill people is so against our ideas. They say the men who were on the Jury to condemn him to death have been so troubled that they have fled to this country, like criminals, although they felt at the time they were doing England a benefit by removing a vain, frivolous tyrant. With Cromwell they find another sort of master, now that he finds himself at the Head of England. I wonder if the English people will long tolerate his rule."

"Mother, how long do you suppose they will keep on hating the Quakers?"

"Oh, Walter, how can I say? They have put a fine on any ship's master now, who dares to bring in a Quaker, that is, in Massachusetts. Now that Mr. Williams has returned from England without the charter, and finds himself really President of Providence Plantations, he himself has advocated punishment of the Quakers for their bad manners. Mr. William Harris is an ardent Quaker, who says that Mr. Williams would like to send them to England. So he wrote to Mr. Williams reminding him of his professing to stand for liberty of Conscience, at which Mr. Williams became very angry."

"Why does he think they have bad manners?"

"Just because they won't take off their hat to him or speak to him as a superior, I suppose."

"I heard them say that a Joseph and Jane Nicholson were sent back to England for being Quakers, that when they arrived there they would not swear on the Bible and so were put in prison. Oh, dear, isn't it dreadful?"

"Well, it is too bad, for false swearing is a sin. They have just passed an act against cursing and swearing, and false witnesses are to receive the punishment intended for the falsely accused. That ought to stop busy-tongued people. I suppose the Quakers' 'Aye' and 'Nay' is as good as an oath."

"So it is, my son."

"I hear Mr. Williams has started to clear the State and Plantations of all his enemies. There has been an order passed by him that any persons found upon examination to be a ringleader of factions or divisions must be sent to England to be tried by the Lord Protector. A small group consisting of Robert West, Catherine Marbury, wife of Richard Scott, Anne Williams and Rebecca Throckmorton, who opposed all authority—otherwise Quakers—were brought to his attention.

"Thomas Harris, William Wigendon and Thomas Angell are accused as ringleaders in the Colony. Mr. Williams also accused Mr. William Harris, Quaker, of high treason because his 'conscience prompted him to not yield subjection to any human order amongst men.' This accusation he has sent to Dr. John Clarke in England, to forward to Cromwell's legal advisors. This Dr. Clarke very wisely has not done. It seems that Mr. Williams is expecting Cromwell to deal directly with the Quakers in Rhode Island!"

Introducing William Vaughan

W M. VAUGHAN OF CAERNEASTHEN, Wales, was
a Doctor of Civil Law, poet and scholar of
distinction. Mr. Vaughan had published a book
hoping to create more interest in colonizing America. He himself, had attempted to plant a colony
in Newfoundland.

One day he met with Lord Wm. Alexander and
Mr. William Cranston, cupbearer to the King. Mr.
Vaughan's account of the meeting is told in Lord
Alexander's address to them. In this speech Lord
Alexander speaks of the difficulties both had in
establishing their colonies. Mr. Vaughan's in the
"Southermost part of Newfoundland, Cambrioll"
and his own at New Scotland beyond Cape Breton.
He also speaks of Sir Henry Carty, Lord Baltimore
and Lord Viscount Falkland as bearing the whole
burden of the north of Newfoundland, all hoping
to be reimbursed by Sir Walter Raleigh's Company
when they returned from Guiana. Their problems
were those of today.

"In such abundance doth my native Country of
Scotland overswarm with people that, if new habi-
tations be not suddenly provided for them, as Hives
for Bees, they must either miscarry of want or turn
Drones unprofitable to the Owner, etc."

He speaks of the exhaustion of the soil from long
cultivation; English cloth, known as Golden Fleece,

being out of demand and no longer thought well of "in contempt." "Our tin, lead and coal mines begin to fail. Our woods lately wasted by the Iron-masters." Nothing remained but "fishing — by hook or by crook, by Letters of Mart, by way of reprisals or revenge, or else by Traffick and Commerce with other Nations besides Spaniards."

So, when Wm. Vaughan appeared in Newport, married the Widow Clarke, and later moved on to settle Westerly, it may have been just the Scotch strain filtering down from the Newfoundland of the previous generation, when his namesake Wm. Vaughan did his best by hook and by pen and even by the crook of a shepherd, for Rev. Wm. Vaughan certainly had a little flock of the Second Baptists at Newport.

IN Portsmouth, June 26, 1655, President Williams presented "William Vaughan of Newport, for that contrary to the laws of this colony had taken Mrs. Clarke as his wife." This is in his writing. What could have provoked him to this? Mr. William Vaughan lived beyond the School House Lane where his pond was situated; the Lane South of School House Lane being Clarke's Lane, not far away. He was evidently a man deeply interested in religion, for the following year, 1656, in spite of the accusation, a congregation of twenty-one persons withdrew from the Baptist Church, and formed the Second Baptist Church, calling Rev. William Vaughan to be their pastor. This group withdrew as they objected to the use of the psalmody and the restraint upon the liberty of prophesying. Frances was now Mrs. William Vaughan. At this same time, Walter Clarke took the precaution to have settled upon him "the dwelling house wherein Mrs. Frances Vaughan now lives with the Garden and orchard and grass plat which lie next the sea and before the house. The Barn and the little Barnfield and great Barnfield, the ground called the meadows butting upon Mr. Easton's ground, Mr. Brenton's ground lately bought by Goodman Champlin, Goodman Clinton's land and Mr. Arnold's and sixty acres lying by Marmaduke Ward's land—which housing and woods is declared to be the inheritance of Walter Clarke, and half of the house commonly called the strong Walter house, wherein Goodman Moone now lives, with the land thereto belonging, is to be sold by Mrs. Frances Vaughan to pay debts. The land called the farm, butting upon Mr. Coggeshall's farm and Goodman Bull's, with the swamp butting upon Goodman Bulls, and Marmaduke Ward's meadows is to remain with the said Mrs. Frances Vaughan for the rest of the children which she had by her husband Capt. Jeremiah Clarke. The housing which Captain Cranston now lives in with the land is to be Captain Cranston's. The land which Mr. Arnold bought of Capt. Clarke is to be confirmed by deed of 18th of Jan. 1658.

Signed,

Frances Vaughan   John Cranston
James Barker   Walter Clarke
Guardian

JAMES BARKER
COAT–OF–ARMS

Persecution — Martyrs

THE persecution of the Rhode Island Quakers was tightening. In '57 a law was passed in Massachusetts which forbade any Quaker banished from the Colony to return. If he should return, one ear was to be cut off, the second return would mean the second ear's removal. Any woman Quaker returning should be scourged and imprisoned. The punishment for the third return was the tongue bored with a hot iron and, in '58, banished upon pain of death.

The Rhode Island assembly wrote to Massachusetts: "The freedom of different consciences had been the principal ground of their charter—that this freedom they still prized as the greatest happiness that men can possess in this world."

One afternoon, Mary Cranston, living very near her mother, sat busily knitting while her mother was sitting opposite, resting. They both wore fair muslin caps and kerchiefs so becoming to young fresh faces and to those more care-worn.

"Herodias Gardiner has gone to bear witness for the Quakers, Mary. She was summoned to Weymouth and although her babe is still nursing, she has gone with Mr. Stanton's young daughter. They are to walk the fifty miles and more. It is well the month of May is pleasant, for she will be most wearied with the journey. Mr. Gardiner has given her a home for many years since John Hicks left Newport. They were married Quaker style before witnesses. It would be better if we had uniform laws and customs. Then our enemies could not complain so against our customs. With Mr. Milton in London writing in defense of divorce and everyone taking the law into their own hands we are like to lose our ideas of correct manners," Frances said. "How dreadful to walk so far to be whipped," exclaimed Mary. "That is the Friends' ideas of Blessedness— "Blessed are ye when men shall revile you and persecute you for my sake," said our Lord and Savior." Thus the women discussed the news of the Quakers.

The following week Mrs. Gardiner returned. She had been punished by whipping, so had the right to be called one of the Rhode Island martyrs. She prayed for her tormentors so winningly that great sympathy was aroused. The fact that she had her little babe with her was very touching to the crowd. She was soon to live, with her young children, across the narrow River, in Narragansett Hill Side, not far from Jireh Bull's.

The next Rhode Island Quakers, William Robinson and Marmaduke Stevenson, went to Boston, the following month, in June, taking their winding sheets with them, to "try out the bloody law into death." Then, in July, Thomas Harris from the Barbadoes, came from the Island, moved by the spirit to warn the Boston authorities of "The terrible day of the Lord." The scene must have been rather stormy, as he had to be dragged away from the meeting by the hair of his head. He was then given a beating.

That same fall Mrs. Catherine Scott, sister of Anne Hutchinson and wife of Richard Scott of Providence, travelled to Boston to see the Quaker, Christopher Holder, who had been punished by having his ears cut off. For her kindly visit, because she was of the despised Quaker belief, she was also punished, suffering ten lashes and threatened with death if she returned.

She spoke thus to the Governor, after the threat: "If God call, woe be to us if we come not. I question not but He whom we love will make us not to count our lives dear unto ourselves for the sake of His name."

It is said that the Governor replied: "And we shall be as glad to take away your lives as ye shall be to lay them down."

You may be sure the sight of her lacerated back stirred fierce emotions in her little daughter's breast. The Clarke cousins at Newport heard much of this, as there was such deep sympathy with all the Quakers of Providence and the Island. As soon as warm weather came again, this little Patience Scott, only eleven years old, walked all the way to Boston to bear witness against the spirit of persecution. Even the hard-hearted court was touched, and the child on account of her tender age was told that she would receive no punishment, and was sent home. But she surely raised a strong amount of sympathy for the Quakers. Very soon after that her sister, Mary Scott, who was engaged to marry the poor fellow whose ears had been cropped, accompanied by Hope Clifton and Mrs. Mary Dyer of Newport, arrived in Boston. Mrs. Dyer had returned from England. The three women were warned not to come again to Boston. In spite of this, Mrs. Dyer, courting martyrdom, went again to see Mr. Holder, with Robinson and Stevenson. They were all three put in prison. Mrs. Dyer was described by Governor Winthrop, a few years previously, as "a very proper and fair woman, of a very proud spirit and much given to revelation." The three Quakers were condemned to be hung—Robinson, Stevenson and Mary Dyer.

With some sixty or more soldiers, drums beating so that their words could not be heard—the three walked hand in hand to the Boston Common—their path lined with men, women, boys and girls, some frowning and shaking their fingers at them, others weeping for them. The glow of joy on the faces of the martyrs can be likened to nothing we see today, for these three Quakers were going in a transport of joy to face their Lord and Sovereign, because they would bow the knee to no human king, but felt themselves directly accountable to their God. Such an exalted feeling few people can attain. Even Roger Williams was moved to write of this spirit of the Quakers: "Who are fit to be Kings, Princes, Governors and Judges, masters of ships, of families, indeed, of any place of power or trust, but those walking Gods and Christs and Spirits, even the meanest of the Quakers?" By which we may measure the transfiguring spirit of confidence which transformed their poor bodies. This from a man whose writings are full of his own religious tolerance, yet who at one time was for no religious form whatever.

When the martyrs came to a certain large elm tree they were stopped, and mounting on a ladder, Mr. Robinson and Mr. Stevenson were hung by the neck till dead, from the bough of the tree. They were described as being "cheerful and ruddy." Mrs. Dyer, speaking before her executioners, said: "It is an hour of the greatest joy I can enjoy in this world. No eye can see, no ear can hear, no tongue can speak, no heart can understand the sweet incomes and refreshings of the Spirit of the Lord, which I now enjoy." The bodies of her comrades were hanging beside her, the noose over her own neck, the Reverend John Wilson put his handkerchief over her face, a tender act, but probably to hide her spiritual countenance which was too much for the accusers to watch. Just at this moment, an officer came dashing up, with her reprieve.

Such an anticlimax! The poor soul was not yet to be a martyr. She was allowed to go to Newport with Mr. Dyer, under bond, but she was not to lodge in

Massachusetts, or to speak to anyone. She went to Long Island for a short time, where she was kindly treated by the Dutch.

Benedict Arnold, son of William Arnold of Pawtuxet Plantation, had been made Governor to succeed Mr. Williams. He was living at Newport, on the hill, a self-respecting man of considerable power and ability.

Letters from Dr. Clarke, who was still in England, informed the people in Newport that Cromwell had died, that Richard Cromwell was now the protector, and that so far he had not succeeded in getting a new charter.

1660

WALTER CLARKE had been greatly moved
by the persecutions of these Quakers. Being
a member of the Newport Society of Friends, his
sympathies were deeply concerned, but being
drilled in Peace and Patience, it was not imperative
for him to declaim, as many of the people were
doing in all the sects of religion. This year of 1660
was a very important one for Rhode Island. Mr.
Brenton was chosen President of the Colony.

Massassoit died, the friend of the White Man.
Of the old school we might call him, having the
benefit of the friendship of some of the finest English Pioneers, who, when they first came to America, were full of high and lofty ideas. Alas, being
human, the commercial spirit grew till it became
greed, and Massassoit, with his Indian red-skins,
children in heart, were changing their opinions of
the White Man. Patience was lacking in these new
comers. They were inclined to damn a great deal in
life. Old women were called witches; women and
men were said to have an evil eye which could cast
spells on cows, babies or other persons; Indians
were believed by many to be imps of darkness, a
cursed race. All this showed distraught minds and
lack of education, a return to dark superstition
brought about by the English Revolution; a free-

dom from all sorts of doctrines, a Reign of Individualism. When each one had moments of dark despair and terror it would communicate itself to the neighborhood.

Like a gleam of white light appears Mrs. Mary Dyer, aflame with faith and already a martyr in her own mind. She returned to Boston this year.

"Mother, I have just seen Mr. Dyer. He says his wife is going to Boston again. It will mean her death." Walter had just ridden up to the gate of the garden and found his mother in her sunbonnet, gathering some early dandelion greens. It was May, and the soft, Newport atmosphere felt already like the breath of summer.

"She has been in Shelter Island for six months, and has very secretly journeyed through the Pequots' and Narragansetts' Country to Providence, and is now going to Massachusetts. They don't want to hang her, but she won't leave the State, preferring to try out the law, so that it may be repealed. It is dreadful for her husband. What can one do with such a spirit? They will have to hang her. But who will believe that her faith and courage will be in vain?"

Frances sighed. Her boy was contemplating marriage at this time, so she changed the subject to one nearer his heart.

"My son, your wedding is at hand. I am glad for you. I will give you some wool covers I have made for you, which shall go in Content Greenman's wedding chest, with a bag of lavender. You shall come to our home for your first Saturday dinner that we may see your new happiness."

"It's good of you, Mother, to make these warm covers for us. I know how busy you always are with the cares and duties of your home. It will be strange to live under my own roof. But it is time I took a wife. I am twenty now, you remember, and have been nine years learning the duties of a man. Wish me well, for I am off to hear Mr. Fox. If I haste, I can perhaps get to Wickford to hear the good man preach at Richard Smith's Trading House. It's strange to think he should gather so many people to hear him. Also, he preaches at Jireh Bull's house, which is in the Narragansett country, among the Indians. If the Quakers were not so kind and peaceful, they would never be allowed to live amongst so many savages."

So saying, Walter rode off, to the north of the Island where he could take a ferry, kept by one Almy, which would carry himself and his horse to Wickford. Cantering along the soft road, he came to the Smith Block House. Here he found many people gathering to hear Mr. Fox, who was a calm, strong speaker and gave forth his views on religion with unmistakable clearness, one of which was a direct approach to the Author and Giver of life, with no middle-man to deal with before reaching the Sovereign, no bowing of the head or scraping with the leg to any human authority; peace within to be gained by patient waiting on the Lord, when He would let His Holy Spirit speak through man as His instrument. Mr. Fox told how he had been sent "forth forbidden to put off my hat to any, high or low"; how he was to have no greater respect for rich than poor, for high estate or low estate, and to use the familiar "thee" and "thou" to all alike; not to exchange greetings as he journeyed, or idly chat, but to travel from place to place in a serious, sober, thoughtful way, to deliver the people from idolatry in every form. He loved to talk seated on a hay stack with the people waiting in silence while he contemplated them, waiting for the Spirit to suggest words of wisdom. He made many converts.

Indian Complications

THERE were Indians all about Wickford. They were used to hunting and trapping the furred animals and brought in many fox skins, beaver, raccoon and some deer skins. Roger Williams had for many years a trading post there, which he sold to Mr. Smith before going to England. Also Mr. Williams had an island called Goat Island. The Islands were in great demand for cattle raising, as they were safe from wolves and from two-legged plunderers. Mr. Coddington and Mr. Arnold had bought Conanicut and Dutch Island for live stock. Little by little and more and more the White Men were pushing the Red Men back. William Carpenter and William Arnold at Pawtuxet, Gorton and Green at Warwick were claiming large tracts. Mr. William Harris was having a very dreadful time with Roger Williams over his land. Like Williams, Gorton, John Clarke, and William Coddington, who had gone back to England to try and get their cases put in black and white, Mr. Harris sailed from America, but alas, his ship was taken by the Barbary Corsairs and he was sold as a slave at Algiers, treated cruelly, whipped, threatened, forced to live on a scant supply of bread and water. Mr. Harris, who was seventy years old at the time, was held at high ransom and the letters from him to his wife were very pitiful: he was willing to exchange his lands and all in his possession if he could raise money for his ransom. He was held for ransom of £459-17s., most of which was paid by the Colony of Connecticut.

Mr. Harris was one of many men who felt the Bay to be a natural boundary and as the Colony was so divided it would be safer to be lined up with Connecticut; as Coddington in Newport was in favor of Massachusetts' protection when he found the factions in the different plantations actually at war. Mr. Gorton certainly stirred things up generally in Providence and Warwick as well as in Newport. This excited the Indians and in 1662 Wamsutta, who was Massasoit's son, surnamed Alexander, was summoned to Boston to answer a charge of conspiracy with the Narragansetts against the colony of Plymouth. As he ignored the order sent by Governor Thomas Prince of Boston, the government sent a warrior to deal with a warrior. This time Major Josiah Winslow, accompanied by his soldiers well-armed, went to Mount Hoap across the bay from Rhode Island, where Alexander was encamped. It was necessary to take the Indian Chief by force in order to get him to go to Boston. A very rough thing to do, but they were rough men living in rough days. He was taken ill at Major Winslow's house as a result and was "allowed to return." When he arrived he was in a dying state and died very soon. Some rumors of poisoning were circulated which only added to the bitter feeling of the Indians.

His brother Matacom, surnamed Philip, succeeded him, a tall, commanding, proud young man
of twenty-two. We may easily imagine his hatred of
the English. From all around came Indians to
attend his coronation and to lament over the death
of his brother. It must have alarmed the settlers,
especially the women and children. Quietly and
seriously the Red Men strode along their ancient
paths, from the Narragansett Country, from the
Wampanoags' haunts to the high hilltop of Mount
Hoap, from the surrounding shores came the canoes
paddled so swiftly by the strong, lithe arms. Standing on the high hill Mount Hoap with his blanket
wrapped about him, in silence the young Philip
looked far to the North toward Swansea, where the
White Man lived, across to the shimmering Falls
above Tiverton, home of Captain Church; across to
the low pasture-lands of Portsmouth; his eyes followed the coast of Rhode Island to Newport and
the little opening to the Great Atlantic, just showing between Mr. Brenton's land and the rocky
dumplings at the end of Conanicut—now Mr. Arnold's and Mr. Coddington's pasture-land, over
across to the Narragansett lands—now mortgaged
to the white men. He turned and gazed bitterly at
the Islands — Prudence, Patience, Goat Island,
owned now by Roger Williams. Bitter tears welled
up and a mighty surge of anger arose, sweeping the
whole beautiful scene red before him. His counselors stood beside him watching him with keenest
interest. Would he hold his own? For five years, he

KING PHILIP RECEIVING THE INDIANS AT MOUNT HAUP

One Hundred Thirty-eight

had been selling his lands and now Matapoiset was to be sold to Mr. Brenton for blankets, farming implements and food, for the Indians must eat and be kept warm *to live*.

The Sachems, Watuspaguin, Nimrod, Annawoṅ and Beebe, were his advisors. He felt the need of most careful counsel. It was to be a struggle for existence. He knew; his counselors knew; every Indian knew. Should the arrogant White Man with his fire-arms and fire water exterminate them or should they unite and exterminate every man, woman and child from these settlements!

After the great assembly of Indians had seated themselves around, and the crown had been placed upon Philip's head, the belt put about his waist, then he must speak.

What the words were we do not know, but the lamentations for the dead Wamsutta, which the Indians made, united them in a common grief, and a common grievance against a common foe. Many a nation has united its warring factions to fight an enemy outside its territory. When the great Book of Life shall be revealed and the hidden secrets discovered, what propagandas will be revealed, which over and over in the world's history, the great ones of power have used to keep the nations from falling asunder. Merely by whipping up their people with the fear of attacking enemies, with the promise of great benefits for the victors! Fear and reward! So this yeast lay fermenting for a few years in the hearts of the Indians.

Hannah Scott

IN the meantime Walter Clarke's wife, Content Greenman, had borne him three little children, Mary, Content and Jeremiah, and then she had died, in March, 1666. The little motherless children were cared for by Frances, as any grandmother would naturally wish to help her son in his bereavement. But it was hard for her to have two homes to keep in order. One day, in the following year, Walter announced to Mrs. Vaughan:

"Mother, I have decided to marry Hannah Scott. I know you already love her, for she has proved herself calm amid affliction, she is fair to look upon, and is eager to leave Providence and loves me full well."

"Who would not, my son? Every day you grow more like your father, more as he would wish you to be. You must take me to Providence, for I shall have many things to say to her."

"Gladly, mother. When shall you go! I myself intend to bring her back when the marriage shall be witnessed and that will be soon."

"Perhaps my duty would be more nearly done were I to stay here, Walter, and prepare a small feast for you when you return. Also I should not like to leave your little babes and you yourselves would prefer to voyage alone with each other. So I shall have to wait to give your Hannah a mother's blessing when she comes here to your own home."

And so the new wife found a warm welcome in Newport when she arrived.

Her mother was the famous Catherine Marbury, wife of Richard Scott. His name stands first in the First Notice in the First Book of Town of Providence, called the Long Old Book with Parchment Cover.

"We whose names are hereunder desirous to inhabit in ye towne of Providence do promise to subject ourselves in active or passive obedience to all such orders or agreements as shall be made for publick good of o^r body in an orderly way by the major consent of the present inhabitants maisters of families incorporated together into a towne fellowship and others whom they shall admit with them only in civil things: Richard Scott, Wm. Reynolds, John Warner, Edward Cope, Thomas Angell, Thomas Harris, Francis Weekes, Benedict Arnold, Joshua Winsor, William Wickendon, John Field."

Was she not of good blood from old England? Her grandfather was a famous clergyman, Rev. Francis Marbury of London; her grandmother was a cousin of the poet Dryden. She was a lovely Quaker girl, full of kindness and appreciation. Walter married her in February, 1667.

In October her little daughter Hannah was born. The mothers were expected to have children and increase the population—there was no question on that subject! So she bore four more children, Catherine, Frances, Jeremiah, the second son of that name, who also died young, and Deliverance, making in all eight children. Two sons died when infants, and Walter's line was carried on by his daughters.

The fight with the Quakers was not over, as far as Roger Williams was concerned. It is true that Mrs. Dyer's martyrdom had ended any serious punishments in Massachusetts. They were too shocking to be allowed to continue. But Mr. Williams, as he grew older, never let himself grow weaker, mentally or physically, and so, in 1671, hearing that Mr. Fox was to be in Newport, after a series of fierce fights with his pen and pamphlets, he rowed himself all the way down to Newport to hold a three-day debate with his opponent. Much to his displeasure, however, Mr. Fox did not appear; three of his "lieutenants" took his place, John Burnyeat, John Stubbs and William Edmundson. It was not a worthy fight for Mr. Williams—in fact, they would not fight with him, and their silence provoked him greatly. The feeling was intense at the stand the enemies of the Quakers had taken. It was too soon to have brought up the heated question, too soon after the Newport Quakers had been lashed and punished and hung. As a result many became Quakers.

Mary Clarke, the wife of John Cranston, had now a little son, Samuel Cranston. Both John and Samuel were destined to be governors of Rhode

Island. Also Frances' daughter, Barbara Dungan's husband, James Barker, and her own son, Walter Clarke, were to be governors. Then, her son, Weston, married Mary Easton, the Quaker, daughter of Peter Easton and Anne Coggeshall, both Governors' children. Her youngest daughter, Sarah, married the widower Calib Carr, who was a governor of Rhode Island; so Frances lived in the most exalted state possible for a humble Quaker, and was in constant touch with affairs of state in the most trying times that Rhode Island has ever lived through.

Further Colonization

MANY irons were in the fire at this time. The English were pushing west into Kingstown. The company of English captains were having many councils with the Indian chiefs.

William Vaughan was much interested in the purchase of land further south along the coast. He set out one day in June with his stepsons, young Jeremy Clarke, now a lad of seventeen, and Latham Clarke, fifteen. The air was fresh, not a cloud in the sky. As they sailed across to the mainland a swell of steady waves was breaking in sparkling white along the sandy beach at Narragansett. On by Point Judea they sailed, around the corner—such a dangerous rock point—on by the wonderful fishing-place, Narragansett Pond, and by Matunuck Beach. The south by south-east breeze carried them along swiftly. Before night they arrived at a small settlement.

After some deliberation they rolled up in blankets and slept under the stars. The next morning they approached the settlement, where they were to meet Mr. George Gardiner who had been for many years looking over the lands and negotiating with the Indians. They found him, also Mr. George Webb. The young Clarkes were thrilled indeed to be walking along with these brave, fearless men. In order to deal with the Red Men, Mr. Gardiner had spent much time becoming used to their ways and learning their language,—so much time, indeed, that Mrs. Gardiner, a few years later, asked for a divorce in Newport, claiming that he no longer supported her or his young sons, and that he had left her so many times, in the wild, bleak, rocky lands of Pettaquamscutt, where she was much of the time without the simplest comforts. He had several sons, Benoni, Henry, Nicholas, William, John — and a little daughter. This little girl was the baby whom her mother had carried in her arms when she walked from Newport to Weymouth to be whipped as a Quaker,—a dreadful blow to Mr. Gardiner, as he was the son of a nobleman, in London, and although his hard frontier life had left its lines on his character, he had that pride of family which suffered intensely. His wife, being a Quaker, destined him to have his share of disgrace, for in a very few years, the Commissioners still further sought to weed out the Quakers by investigating his marriage with Herodias. The result was a divorce for "non-support," we should say today. Mrs. Gardiner was soon married to Mr. John Porter who had divorced his wife. He was generous and kind to Herodias and the Gardiner boys, giving them large tracts of land on the Pettaquamscutt Ridge, so that Herodias must have died in a happier condition than she had lived during most of her early life.

Certainly at this time Mr. George Gardiner was

helping the English settlements and on this particular ninth of June, he was full of enthusiasm as he saw the Rev. William Vaughan and the bright, interested faces of the Clarkes. They walked to the Indian place of meeting where Sosoa was found, and with great solemnity bargained and obtained land which is now Westerly. There were eleven Indians of high station, including Wowaloam, the wife of Miantonomi, who was the only woman to sign the deed. Sosoa was the owner of all that tract as Wowaloam declared in a signed statement, thus guaranteeing the title of right of sale to the Newport men and their associates. The place had been called Misguanicutt.

Beside Mr. George Webb and Mr. George Gardiner were Mr. William Vaughan and Robert Stanton, who had come to Newport at the same time that George Gardiner came and who was his friend, at whose home he had married Herodias Long Hicks, according to the Quaker way—without magistrate or minister, merely by stating before witnesses their matrimonial intentions. Very few marriages were recorded or solemnized by clergy before 1700. Also in this group of White Men were John Fairfield, Hugh Mosher and James Longbottom, from Newport. We may imagine the sombre scene as the silent Indians gravely rose, one by one, from the circle of the council. First, Sosoa signed, with fingers unaccustomed to hold a pen—his only mark being a vertical line. He probably was very sorry to sell his land, but very much influenced by the fear of the Pequots and the desire to line his people with the clever white folk. After he had returned to his seat, the Clarkes witnessed his signature, young Jeremy and Latham, and Henry Clarke, as relatives of William Vaughan. Next came Awashwash, making a mark much as a child beginning to write a W. Then the interpreter Indian, Nucum, wrote WO. George Webb and George Gardiner followed with much solemnity. These deeds were made as impressive as possible, so that the Red Men should remember the land transaction for generations. The Indians Cachaquant, Sammecat, Passicus, Wowaloam, Avashous, Poatoch, Unkaguant and Ne-O-Wam confirmed the deed, and the right of Sosoa to bargain and to sell to the White Men.

This accomplished, the Clarkes returned to Newport and the following year their stepfather, William Vaughan, headed a petition to the Providence Plantations assembled at Portsmouth. His sons-in-law, James Barker and John Cranston and Caleb Carr, also signed the petition pertaining to the Westerly land. Possibly they thought of starting a new colony there, but evidently, as affairs became more settled, they all remained in Newport.

Along the eastern shore of the Narragansett County, with an idea of raising cattle there, Capt. Atherton, Capt. John Brown and Capt. Thomas Willett, with others, debated patiently and in a

One Hundred Forty-eight

friendly way with Nenigrat, Quequakanuit, Suc-
quansk, Coguinaguand, and Schutup, the Indian
Chiefs, and finally had paid the five hundred feet of
wampum as a mortgage on the land, to be called
Boston Neck. We can picture these White captains,
Atherton being the most military in action, Brown
and Willett being the conciliatory type, always having been on friendly terms with the Indians. They
sat around the circle with the Sachems who, strong,
well-greased, smoky-eyed, emitted grunts of approval or maintained deep silence while the various
points to be settled were stated to them by Captain
Willett. Several meetings were held before the final
amount of the mortgage was paid.

We must remember that the greatest impression
could be produced on the Indian only by White
Men who were conquerors. They must be only the
bravest and most victorious—a weak man was con-
temptible to their way of thinking. So the talk had
to do with the great, unknown King across the ocean,
and the service due him. Charles II had at last raised
enough money, pride and courage to leave France.
In October, 1660, he landed at Dover and, march-
ing to London, was proclaimed King. Then it was
that the crowd turned against the dead Cromwell.
He was taken from the grave and his head put upon
a pike as a traitor. All of which shows that it makes a
great difference how you look at things. The mother
country had been through a terrible experience; its
revolution had upset all rule along the line. Though

not as bloody as the French or the Russian revolutions, we must, in justice, compare it with these and line up, cruel as it seems, those who destroyed and demolished the ruling order, smashing the works of art and beauty as if they were heathen idols, and with pious zeal destroying priceless treasures of centuries in order to replace them all with what they felt was Truth and Righteousness. They were like a father, who filled with righteous wrath destroys the good as well as the evil in his blind passion for the Lord. There was, however, that great and fine desire to enlighten the Savages, who were far different from the Indians today. In comparing these, we cannot fail to see how modern methods differ. England lets the Hindoos alone, and France, the Mohammedans, when it comes to their religions. Time will tell which is better; certainly the modern way seems to have left them as they have been throughout the centuries, and a traveller can notice the difference between a Mohammedan and a Christian civilization.

War Clouds – 1675

THE Judgment of the Lord, prophesied by Mr. Easton, was preparing to descend upon the Plantations. Naturally even the Quaker mothers became alarmed. But their faith in kindness conquering the savage instincts held them calm.

In June '75 word came to Newport that King Philip was planning an uprising. A messenger was sent by ferry at the north of Rhode Island to make arrangements for a conciliatory meeting with the Indians. The messenger was at first turned away, the Indians refusing to listen, and not until they found he came from the Island, were they willing to meet the delegation.

Philip was proud, unarmed, but surrounded by forty armed Indians. There were to be no chances taken with this Chief. What a contrast was the Newport delegation, — five Englishmen, headed by Deputy Governor John Easton, a Quaker and a Peace-maker. We thank him for the notes, taken without the aid of the dictionary:—

"We sat very friendly together — we told (Philip) our object was to indever that they might not reseve or do Rong.

"They said that was well.

"They had dun no Rong—the English ronged them.

"We said we knew the English, and the Indians ronged them, and the Indians said the English ronged them, but our Desire was the quarrel might rightly be desided in the best way and not as dogs desided their quarrells. The Indians owned yt fighting was the worst way: then they propounded how right might take place. We replied 'Arbitration'."

This little friendly talk had but a temporary effect in checking the revenge planned so long and carefully by the Indians. We must remember that France, England and Holland had been at war; that probably Philip had been tempted to harass the English Colony, and that it was customary generally, at that time, to use the Indians to harass the enemy settlers.

War

THE firebrand was the signal. It first lighted the dark night of fear and terror in the hearts of the Colonial mothers at Swansea, when two houses were burned on June 20th. Four days later, nine or ten settlers were killed in a skirmish. Massachusetts ordered affairs in the Plantations. They asked Roger Williams to go, with some of their men, including Capt. Edward Hutchinson, to try and make peace with the Narragansetts. Mr. Williams felt so uneasy about their attitude that he advised a Council of War to be held in each of the towns after his interview with the Narragansetts.

In the meantime, Rhode Island was asked for boats to patrol the coast. Benjamin Church of Tiverton was given charge by Governor Winslow to attend to this. Capt. Church was on good terms with the Sakonnet Indians, whose queen, Awashonks, was inclined to be friendly with the White traders.

Newport and Portsmouth had a relay crew of men patrolling the coast, day and night, by boats.

The Massachusetts and Plymouth troops descended on Philip at Mt. Hope and drove him back to Pocasset. As he retreated, he left a path of burning houses, with a head or hand of the poor unfortunate man of the house stuck on a pole, to warn the neighborhood. Capt. Thomas Willetts' son, Jeremiah, was thus killed by some Indians, not knowing who he was. Later, the head was returned with deep sorrow, covered with flowers, as Philip had ordered Thomas Willetts' and John Brown's family spared "for their kindness." How pathetic! It might all have been different if there had been more "kindness."

When Frances, in Newport, heard of this she could not refrain from comparing this episode to the retreat of Matilda from Burgundy, when she married Clovis. As she passed out of her native land, which had been taken from her father by his cruel brother, Matilda left a wide path of burning and pillaging which told her uncle of her deep offense at his injustice in taking her father's—Chilperic's—lands. "Fire and destruction." "Revenge——!"

Frances was deeply concerned at these wars and had the mother's task of being calm and cheerful when John Cranston was appointed, "April 11,

Twenty-seven men stayed in Providence to protect it from the Indians.

R. Williams	Tho. and Jack Field	M. John Angel
Tho Fenner	Tho. Clements	Thos Arnold
John Morey	Wm. Hopkins	Ephraim Pray
James Olney	John Rodes	Jos. Woodward
Jo. Whipple	Thos. Wallen	Ed Binnet
James Angelo	Nath. Waterman	Wm. Lancaster
Richard Pray	Henry Ashton	Wm. Hawkings
Abraham Pray	Dan Abbot	Sam Mason
	Val. Whitman	

Early Record of Town of Providence.

1676, Major and Chief Captain of all the Colony forces." As her own sons were Quakers and opposed to all the force of War, she was somewhat divided in her feeling. She could not help feeling pride in her Scotch son-in-law as he marched away with his men to join the Massachusetts soldiers. He was going to defend their homes and, in fact, the English Settlements. Captain John Gorham after the Swamp Fight reported that he had lost thirty of his men and over forty were wounded. He himself was so badly wounded that he died the following year.

Major Cranston came back safely and was made Governor of Rhode Island from 1678-80, when he died. Fifty-four is not so old in years, but what a record of service, to be continued through his son and Mary's son, in the life of Samuel Cranston. Well might Frances be proud of her children and grand-children and well might her children and grand-children be grateful to her constant devotion and untiring efforts to build men and women worthy to direct this new Country. This was constantly in the minds of the settlers. The living for the generations to come, on the highest standard of Christian Civilization. These people who came from the Old World sick and suffering from Wars and Pestilence and Intolerance and Slavery to make a great experiment. The great experiment in the New World, whether in New France, New Scotland, New England, New Netherlands of New Spain!

Dr. John Clarke had returned with the Charter,

a marvelous great document with a wonderful fig-
urehead of Charles II depicted on it in all his curls.
This Charter is actually made out "to our good
friend, John Clarke, and his associates," followed
by a list of the prominent men of the Plantations
very pleasantly mingled. We can see the kind sug-
gestion of Dr. Clarke. It included all the factions,—
Roger Williams and Coddington, too. Captain Baxter brought the Charter to the Rhode Island men
amid great rejoicing. He was the same man who had
been implicated with Mr. Coddington when their
enemies attempted to make them appear conspira-
tors with the Dutch against England.

Amid the distress, with fire and pillage at Warwick, Providence, Pawtuxet, Swansea and Narragansett, many women were dying of fright and little
babies were being born without a chance to live, in
the haste and exposure. These were sad days for the
Colonial women. Dear old Mr. Coddington stood
on the shore to receive the frightened women and
children who came to Newport for refuge. Of
course, Newport and the Quakers were blamed this
time for not furnishing protection to the Plantations. Captain Arthur Fenner provoked Mr. Walter
Clarke, Quaker, to make this statement.

"We know the Lord's hand is against New England, and no weapon formed will or shall prosper
till the work be finished by which the wheat is pulled
up with the tares and the innocent suffer with the
guilty."

We certainly know that Governor Walter Clarke read his Bible. He was now thirty-eight, and a firm friend of Mr. Coddington, now over seventy. Mr. Coddington had married for the third wife, Anne, the sister of Frances Brinley, a member of a fine old English family who had recently come to Newport. Coddington was still proud of his Island Colony and forgetful of his hard lessons and troubles, he determined to save this new experiment with all his might.

The Rhode Island Assembly sent letters advising the people of the mainland to come to the Island, as it was best protected. Those were busy days and nights, for they came in pitiful condition, always of course by boat, from all over the shores of the Bay and Providence. Those of the Newport and Portsmouth people who were not willing, were compelled by the Quakers to give hospitality to the refugees. Land was given to them to plant, and they were permitted to keep their cows on the Common. The little homes were filled to overflowing with the women and little children, the refugees from Providence, Warwick and Pawtuxet. Of course Frances was foremost in her charitable hospitality and as calmly as possible superintended the many added cares of her household, quieting the worried women as best she could.

Five hundred and forty men from Massachusetts, armed and equipped for war, marched across the Plantations. They were joined by one hundred

GOVERNOR CODDINGTON AND QUAKERS OF NEWPORT GIVING
REFUGE TO THE WOMEN AND CHILDREN OF THE PROVIDENCE,
PAWTUXET AND WARREN PLANTATIONS

One Hundred Fifty-eight

and fifty-eight men from Connecticut and some volunteers from Rhode Island. All met at Tower Hill, south of Wickford, not far from Richard Smith's Block House. They started to drive the Indians to a corner somewhere and burn them out. Led by Nathaniel Davenport and Isaac Johnson, they were met by the Narragansetts and driven back. A fresh company of volunteers, men with homes and families to protect, tried to end the conflict. By this time the Indians were in the great swamp back of Kingston. It was in December; the days were short; darkness came all too soon, and the men were terribly tired with the effort of walking through the woods, their eyes and ears alert for every trembling leaf or creaking, crackling branch which might mean an arrow in their heart. The Indians were determined to protect their winter supplies, though, and had hidden their possessions in a block house in this wild marsh. Here the Colonists arrived at last, on the verge of exhaustion, cold and hungry. They were enheartened by the arrival of Major Samuel Appleton with his troops. With supreme effort they advanced through the foreguard. With howls and hoots and great confidence they broke into the fort, followed by the Connecticut men. It was a hand to hand encounter now—musket butts and tomahawks, merciless and bloody. Then they set fire to the Block House. What an indescribable scene! What screams and sounds of anguish—a horrible retribution for the burning of the White man's houses at Providence,

Warwick, Pawtuxet, Swansea, Jereh Bull's house at Narragansett. Like rats in a nest, the Indians were burned. It is probable that between one hundred and one hundred fifty Indians were killed, and as many disabled. Over three hundred warriors were taken prisoner and almost as many squaws with their children.

The painful journey back that night cannot be imagined. Feet wet from the marsh, scratched and torn by the brambles, they had many miles to go before they could rest. No knowing what might arrive if they paused; chilled numb were their hands, but they must finish the work begun. There were over sixty of their own soldiers killed. These were taken to Richard Smith's house at Wickford and buried in a common grave. No time for more ceremony. The wounded, about one hundred and fifty, were then taken to Newport, also the Indians to be tried for murder, and some were taken to Providence to be sold as slaves. Here again Frances had to help nurse the sick men.

Through these days on the Island the Quaker influence was shining like a clear light in the darkness. There were to be no slaves, that was the Quaker opinion. To avoid any trouble, they kept the young Indians as servants, making a law that all "Indian servants of 12 years old and upward should be provided with an attendant in the daytime, and be locked up at night, but no Indian in this Colony shall be a slave save only for debts covenant and as if they had been countrymen not in war." The captive Indians, men, women and children, were sold as slaves in Massachusetts and Plymouth. Roger Williams himself heads the list of names in Providence of the townsmen who effected bond sales of the poor unfortunate Red Men, his former friends.

Newport at this time was the only Colony in what is now the State of Rhode Island, which was unmolested by the Indians. It was the Island of Refuge and Peace. Now with these poor maimed soldiers there was much extra work to be done in bandaging and cleansing the mud-stained wounds, in cooling the fevered brow, for after the exhaustion and chill came the racking fevers. These duties of nursing came instinctively to the Quaker women. They knew how to brew the nourishing porridge and broths, and as soon as possible, get their rugged guests on their feet and off to their own homes.

The prison at Newport was filled with the most vicious of the Indians. The poor captives were nearly crazed with hunger, cold, fear; tormented by their own misery and despised by their captors. The day came for their trial. Some of these Indians had been brought to Newport by Roger Williams' son from Providence in his sloop. Walter Clarke was at this time Governor of Rhode Island and President of the Court. He could not, and would not judge those poor unfortunate Indians. He did not go to the trial, which took place without him. His brother Latham was present as a member of the

THE TRIAL OF QUINNAPIN BY LATHAM CLARKE, ROGER
WILLIAMS, ARTHUR FENNER, RANDALL HOLDEN
AND OTHERS

Court Martial at Newport. Roger Williams, an old man now, sat also in judgment with Arthur Fenner, Randall Holden, who later married Frances Dungan, William Harris and others. The husband of Queen Weetamo, named Quinnapin, was one of the prominent Indians condemned to death.

The Chief Canonchet had met with a much more horrible fate at the hands of his treacherous Red Skin enemies. He had been warned by young Robert Stanton but had proudly turned from him calling him "Much child." He was shot by the Pequots; the Mohegans cut off his head and quartered his body; the Nonnighats built a fire and burned his body, taking his head to the English rulers in Hartford "as a token of their love and fidelity to the English."

The colonies could not feel safe as long as King Philip still was in hiding, for he had a tremendous power over the Indians, and although the scouts and Indian fighters were busy searching the woods, they had not yet found him. Captain Benjamin Church of Tiverton was one of these men. It was he alone who made a peaceful agreement with Queen Awashonks of the Sakonnet Tribe of Indians. Carrying a bottle of rum and a roll of tobacco, he went to call on the Queen. She was a vain woman, spending much time on her personal adornment, we are told. They sat down in the tall grass to talk, when suddenly on all sides arose armed Indians. Captain Church bravely asked them to lay aside their weapons. Then, passing the bottle of rum and tobacco, he had his friendly chat, which succeeded in binding the Sakonnets to the English and breaking with Philip's Wampanoags. This was earlier. Now this same man appears on the Island as an Indian Scout, having ranged the woods and swamps on an awful search for stray Indians. It was in August that he captured Philip's pitiful wife and nine year old son. These were both sold as slaves in the islands in the South, far from their home. Mrs. Church and the Captain's children were staying on Rhode Island in Major Sanford's home, well sheltered. Captain Church was seized with a wild longing to see them. He went just as he was, his face stained, his hair wild, arrayed like an Indian that he might more easily find Philip. Rather forgetful of his appearance, he entered Major Sanford's home and rushed to embrace his wife. It is not surprising to know that she fainted at sight of him.

As he was trying to restore her to consciousness, the sound of horses hoofs came to their ears and soon in the doorway appeared Major Sanford; Captain Golding was with him.

"Philip is back at Mount Haup Neck," they told Church.

Without further delay the Captain set out to catch him. Church had with him this time an Englishman, Caleb Cook, and a friendly Indian named Alderman. They both fired as they discovered a group of Indians in the woods. Among them was

King Philip. They had all started to run, but Philip
stumbled and fell as the bullet from Alderman's
musket hit him.

He was dressed only in his small breeches and
stockings, his musket in his hand. He fell face down
in the mud and water. Captain Church described
the poor hunted monarch thus:

"A doleful great naked dirty beast he looked
like." How tragic—one might imagine—
Those berries bright, all bloody red
So sharply to our eyes relate—
"Here dreadful deeds, here blood was shed
Here warriors once encountered hate."
A witness through the winter long
That Murder cannot right a wrong—
You who pick these berries red
Please say a prayer for the Red Man dead.

With the capture, Anawon, Philip's Chief Captain who had been a counselor to Massassoit, gave
the crown, belts, and gorge of King Philip to Captain Church. He was now the Conqueror. He had
conquered the highest chief left. These emblems
of Royalty were later given by the Governor of
Plymouth to King Charles II, as the ruler of the
colonies.

Charles II ordered a reprieve from all persecution of the Quakers. They had given a haven of
refuge to the hunted settlers at their homes in
Newport, which should never be forgotten.

Frances Latham Dungan Clarke Vaughan, lived

through all this excitement, a wonderful and interesting epoch in our history. She died September, 1677. Her husband, the worthy Reverend William Vaughan, died the same year. Mrs. Vaughan was buried in the Governor's Burying Ground in Newport. On her gravestone was written:—

"Here lyeth ye body of
Mrs. Frances Vaughan
alias Clarke ye mother
of ye only children of
Capt. Jeremiah Clarke
She dyed ye I week in
September 1677 in ye 67th
year of her age."

Self effacing, like the spiritual forces, hard to visualize—felt, not visible.

The wonderful Quakers have never had their proper place in the History of Rhode Island. If one drives about the State, though, one may still see their Meeting Houses, quiet witnesses of their quiet influence at Narragansett, at Woonsocket, at Saylesville, at Providence on Meeting Street, at Portsmouth on the top of the long hill, at Newport in the centre of the old district. With the men and boys on one side of the room—the women and girls on the other side—wearing long hooded bonnets so that their bright eyes might not rove over to the other side during the long periods of silence, they would sit quietly waiting for the Spirit to move them. Here, today, in the rush and turmoil of our complicated existence, at the head of the most pacific

Nation in the world, sits in the most exalted seat of our Government, for the first time in its history, a Quaker—Mr. Hoover, calm, deliberate, disarming, patient, alone and unshaken. The new Quaker Meeting House in Washington is an emblem of simplicity and nobility of thought which enshrines a group of worshippers who feel confident to deal directly with the most exalted of all rulers, their King and Savior.

May this spirit of peace and calm faith pervade our land, as the yeast leavens the loaf of bread!

To the Quakers in Rhode Island who held out so bravely through their persecutions and actually saved the State, let us give credit for their consistent construction to our National Life.

List of Nova Scotia Baronets

(Campbell—The Scotman in Canada)

1625 May 28   Gordon of Gordon (Sir Robert)
Premier Bt.   *Nova Scotia*
Strachan of Strachan   *New Brunswick*
Keith, Earl Marischal   *New Brunswick*

May 29   Campbell of Glenurchy (Marquess
of Breadalbane)   *Anticosti*
Innis of New Innis (Duke of
Roxburgh)   *Anticosti*
Wemyss of New Wemyss (Earl of
Wemyss)   *Anticosti*

May 30   Livingston of Dunipace   *New Brunswick*
Douglas of Douglas   *New Brunswick*

July 14   Macdonald of Macdonald (Lord
Macdonald)   *New Brunswick*

July 19   Murray of Cockpool (Earl Mans-
field)   *New Brunswick*

Aug. 30   Colquhoun of Colquhoun   *Nova Scotia*

Aug. 31   Gordon of New Cluny (Marquess of
Huntly)   *New Brunswick*

Sept. 1   Lesly of Lesly   *New Brunswick*

Sept. 2   Gordon of New Lesmure   *New Brunswick*

Sept. 3   Ramsay of Ramsay   *New Brunswick*

Nov. 17   Forester of Corstorphine (Earl
Verulam   *Nova Scotia*

Dec. 28   Erskine of Erskine   *Anticosti*
Graham of Braco   *Anticosti*
Hume of Palworth   *Anticosti*

One Hundred Sixty-nine

1626	Mar. 30	Forbes of Forbes	*New Brunswick*
	Mar. 31	Johnston of Johnston	*New Brunswick*
	Apr. 21	Burnett of Leys Burnett	*New Brunswick*
	Apr. 22	Moncrieff of Moncrieff	*New Brunswick*
	Apr. 24	Ogilvie of New Carnnosie	*New Brunswick*
	May 1	Gordon of Lochinvar (Viscount Kenmore)	*New Brunswick*
	June 1	Murray of Murray	*New Brunswick*
	July 18	Blackadder of Blackadder	*Anticosti*
	Sept. 29	Ogilvy of Ogilvy, Innerquharity	*New Brunswick*
1627	Mar. 18	Mackay of Reay (Lord Reay)	*Anticosti*
	Mar. 28	Maxwell of Mauldslie	*New Brunswick*
	Mar. 28	Stewart of Bute (Marquess of Bute)	*New Brunswick*
	Apr. 18	Stewart of Corswall (Earl of Galloway)	*New Brunswick*
	May 2	Napier of Napier (Lord Napier)	*New Brunswick*
	June 25	Livingston of Kennaird (Earl of Newburgh)	*Anticosti*
	July 4	Cunningham of Cunninham	*Anticosti*
	July 17	Carmichael of Carmichael	*Nova Scotia*
	July 19	McGill of McGill	*Anticosti*
	July 20	Ogilvy of Banff (Lord Banff)	*New Brunswick*
	Oct. 18	Johnston of New Elphinstone	*New Brunswick*
	Nov. 21	Cockburn of Cockburn	*New Brunswick*
	Dec. 13	Campbell of Lundie-Campbell	*Anticosti*
		Campbell of Aberuchill	*Anticosti*
1628	Jan. 1	Acheson of Monteagle (Earl Gosford)	*Anticosti*
	Jan. 10	Sandilands of Sandilands (Lord Torpichen)	*Anticosti*

	Jan. 10	Montgomery of New Skilmorly (Earl of Eglinton)	*Anticosti*
	Jan. 12	Haliburton of Pitcur	*Anticosti*
		Campbell of New Auckinbreck	*Anticosti*
		Innis of Balveny	*Nova Scotia*
	Jan. 14	Campbell of New Ardnamurchan	*Anticosti*
	Feb. 19	Hope of Craighall	*Anticosti*
	Feb. 22	Skene of Curriehill	*New Brunswick*
		Preston of Preston Airdrie	*New Brunswick*
		Gibson of Durie	*Anticosti*
	May 14	Crawford of Kilbirnie	*Anticosti*
		Riddell of New Riddell	*Anticosti*
	May 15	Murray of Blackbarony	*Anticosti*
	May 16	Murray of Elibank Murray (Lord Elibank)	*Anticosti*
	May 21	Cadell of Cadell	*Anticosti*
		Mackenzie of Tarbat (Earl of Cromarty)	*Anticosti*
	June 20	Elphinstone of New Glasgow	*New Brunswick*
	Sept. 29	Forbes of Castle-Forbes (Earl Granard)	*Nova Scotia*
		Hamilton of Killach (Down) (Marquess of Abercorn)	*Nova Scotia*
	Oct. 2	Stewart of Ochiltree (Earl of Castle-Stewart)	*Nova Scotia*
		Barrett, Lord Newburgh	*New Brunswick*
1629	June 26	Bruce of Stenhouse	*New Brunswick*
		John Nicholson of Lasswade	*Anticosti*
		Arnot of Arnot	*Anticosti*
	June 28	Oliphant of Oliphant	*Anticosti*
		Agnew of Agnew	*Nova Scotia*
		Keith of Ludquhairn	*Nova Scotia*
	Nov. 30	St. Estienne of La Tour	*Nova Scotia*

1630	Mar. 31	Hannay of Mochrum	*New Brunswick*
	Apr. 20	Forbes of New Craigievar	*New Brunswick*
	Apr. 24	Stewart (Lord Ochiltree)	*New Brunswick*
		Crosbie	*New Brunswick*
		Crosbie of Crosbie Park Wickland	
			New Brunswick
	May 12	St. Estienne of St. Denniscourt	*Nova Scotia*
	July 24	Sibbald of Rankeillor Sibbald	*Anticosti*
	Oct. 2	Murray of New Dunearn	*New Brunswick*
	Nov. 13	Richardson of Pencaithland,	*New Brunswick*
	Nov. 25	Maxwell of Pollock	*Nova Scotia*
		Cunningham of New Robertland,	
			Nova Scotia
1631	Mar. 5	Wardlaw of Wardlaw	*Nova Scotia*
	June 2	Sinclair of Canisby (Earl of Caith-	
		ness) .	*Anticosti*
	June 18	Gordon of New Embo	*Anticosti*
	Sept. 3	McLean of Movaren	*Anticosti*
1633	Dec. 22	Balfour of Denmiln	*Cape Breton*
	Dec. 25	Cunningham of Auchinharvie	*Cape Breton*
1634	June 7	Vernat of Carington (Yorkshire),	
			Cape Breton
		Bingham of Castle bar (Mayo) (Earl	
		of Lucan)	*Cape Breton*
		Munro of Foulis	*Cape Breton*
		Foulis of Colinton	*Cape Breton*
1635	Jan 6	Hamilton of Hamilton (Lord Bel-	
		haven)	*Cape Breton*
	June 8	Gascoine of Barnhow (Yorkshire),	
			Cape Breton
	June 18	Norton of Chestone (Suffolk)	*Cape Breton*
	June 29	Pilkington of Stainlie (Yorkshire),	
			Cape Breton
	Sept. 26	Widdrington of Cairntington	
		(Northumberland)	*Cape Breton*

	Dec. 10	Hay of Smithfield	*Cape Breton*
	Dec. 19	Bolles of Cudworth (Notts)	*Cape Breton*
		Raney of Rutain (Kent)	*Cape Breton*
1636	Feb. 17	Fortesque of Salden (Bucks)	*Cape Breton*
	Feb. 20	Thomson of Duddlington	*Cape Breton*
	June 17	Browne of Neale (Mayo) (Lord Kilmaine)	*Cape Breton*
	June 18	More of Longford (Notts)	*Cape Breton*
		Abercrombie of Birkenbog	*Cape Breton*
		Sinclair of Stevenson	*Cape Breton*
		Curzon-Keddlestone (Derbysh.) (Lord Scardale)	*Cape Breton*
	Nov. 21	Bailie of Lochead	*Cape Breton*
1637	Jan. 16	Nicholson of Carnock (Thomas Nicholson)	*Cape Breton*
	Mar. 13	Preston of Valleyfield	*Cape Breton*
	July 31	Ker of Greenhead	*Cape Breton*

1638   Pollock of Jordanhill,
       Musgrave of Hayton Castle,

1639   Turing of Foveran,

1642   Gordon of Haddo (Earl of Aberdeen),

1646   Hamilton of Silverton Hill,

1648   Seton of Abercorn,

1651   Primrose of Chester (Earl of Rosebery),

1663   Carnegy of Southesk,
       Hay of Park,

1664   Murray of Stanhope,
       Dalrymple of Stair (Viscount Stair),
       Sinclair of Longformacus,

1665   Purves (Hum Campbell) of Purves,
       Malcolm of Balbeadie,

1666	Menzies of that Ilk,
	Dalzell of Glencoe (Earl of Carnwath),
	Erskine of Alva (Earl of Rosslyn),
	Erskine of Cambo (Earl of Mar and Kellie),
	Wood of Boyentown,
	Elliot of Stobs,
	Ramsay of Banff,
1667	Shaw-Stewart of Greenock,
	Don of Newton,
	Douglas of Kelhead (Marquess of Queensberry)
1668	Barclay of Pierston,
1669	Wallace of Craigie,
	Cunyngham of Caprington (now Dick-Cunyngham
	Baronet of Preston Field),
1671	Halkett of Pitfirrave,
	Cockburn of that Ilk,
	Home of Blackadder,
	Scott of Ancrum,
1672	Cunningham of Corsehill,
	Ross of Balnagowan,
	Jardine of Applegirth,
1673	Murray of Ochertyre,
	Mackenzie of Coul,
1675	Hamilton of Preston,
1679	Clerk of Penicuik,
	Cochrane of Ochiltree (Earl of Dundonald),
1680	Baird of Saughton Hall,
	Dundonald,
	Baird of Saughton Hall,
	Maitland of Hatton (Earl of Lauderdale),
1681	Maxwell of Montreath,
1682	Maxwell of Pollock,
	Kennedy of Culzean (Marquess of Ailsa),
	Bannerman of Elsick,

1683   Stewart of Grandtully,
        Pringle of Stitchel,
        Maxwell of Sprinkell,
        Seton of Pitmedden,
1685   Grierson of Lag,
        Kilpatrick of Closeburn,
        Laurie of Maxwelton,
        Dalzell of Brims,
        Montcrieff of that Ilk,
1686   Broun of Colstoun,
        Kinlock of Gilmerton,
        Nicholson of Tillicoultry,
        Gordon of Park,
1687   Calder of Muirton,
        Stuart of Allanbank,
        Hall of Dunglas,
        Thriepland of Fingask,
1688   Dick-Lauder of Fountainhall,
        Grant of Dalvey,
1693   Stewart of Coltness,
        Dunbar of Durn,
1698   Dalrymple of North Berwick,
        Dalrymple of Cousland (Viscount Stair)
1700   Mackenzie of Gairloch,
        Forbes of Foveran,
        Livingstone of Westquarter,
1700   Johnstone of Westerhall,
        Elliot of Minto (Earl of Minto),
        Dunbar of Northfield,
1702   Cunninghame of Milncraig,
        Grant-suttie of Balgone,
1703   Mackenzie of Scatwell,
        Cathcart of Carleton,
        Ferguson of Kilkerran,
        Reid of Barra,
        Hay of Alderston,

1704   Murray of Melgun (Count Murray)
       Wemyss of Bogie,
       Grant of Grant (Earl of Seafield)
       Sinclair of Dunbeath,
       Wedderburn of Blackness,

1705   Grant of Monymusk,
       Holbourne of Kirshie,

1706   Gordon of Earlston,
       Naesmith of Posso,
       Dunbar of Hempriggs (Lord Duffus),

1707   Dick of Preston Field (also Baronet of Capington),
       Stewart of Tillycoultry,
       Cragie of Gairsay.

An Early Syndicate

Names of the Council for Fishing formed 1629. Isle of Lewis, headquarters.

Scotch· Wm , Earl of Morton, Wm., Earl of Strathern, Robert, Earl of Roxburgh; Wm., Viscount of Sterline; John Hay, Esq. and George Fletcher, Esq.

English Richard, Lord Weston; Thomas, Earl of Arendell and Surry, Philip, Earl of Pembroke; Thomas, Viscount Savage, Francis, Lord Cottington, and Sir John Cooke.

CPSIA information can be obtained at www.ICGtesting.com
Printed in the USA
LVOW08*0806020416

481890LV00008B/32/P